Editor-in-Chief and Founder:
Lyndon H. LaRouche, Jr.
Editorial Board: *Lyndon H. LaRouche, Jr. , Helga Zepp-LaRouche, Paul Gallagher, Tony Papert, Gerald Rose, Dennis Small, Jeffrey Steinberg, William Wertz*
Co-Editors: *Paul Gallagher, Tony Papert*
Managing Editor: *Nancy Spannaus*
Technology: *Marsha Freeman*
Books: *Katherine Notley*
Graphics: *Alan Yue*
Photos: *Stuart Lewis*
Circulation Manager: *Stanley Ezrol*

INTELLIGENCE DIRECTORS
Counterintelligence: *Jeffrey Steinberg, Michele Steinberg*
Economics: *John Hoefle, Marcia Merry Baker, Paul Gallagher*
History: *Anton Chaitkin*
Ibero-America: *Dennis Small*
Russia and Eastern Europe: *Rachel Douglas*
United States: *Debra Freeman*

INTERNATIONAL BUREAUS
Bogotá: *Miriam Redondo*
Berlin: *Rainer Apel*
Copenhagen: *Tom Gillesberg*
Houston: *Harley Schlanger*
Lima: *Sara Madueño*
Melbourne: *Robert Barwick*
Mexico City: *Gerardo Castilleja Chávez*
New Delhi: *Ramtanu Maitra*
Paris: *Christine Bierre*
Stockholm: *Ulf Sandmark*
United Nations, N.Y.C.: *Leni Rubinstein*
Washington, D.C.: *William Jones*
Wiesbaden: *Göran Haglund*

ON THE WEB
e-mail: eirns@larouchepub.com
www.larouchepub.com
www.executiveintelligencereview.com
www.larouchepub.com/eiw
Webmaster: *John Sigerson*
Assistant Webmaster: *George Hollis*
Editor, Arabic-language edition: *Hussein Askary*

EIR (ISSN 0273-6314) *is published weekly (50 issues), by EIR News Service, Inc., P.O. Box 17390, Washington, D.C. 20041-0390. (703) 777-9451*

European Headquarters: E.I.R. GmbH, Postfach Bahnstrasse 9a, D-65205, Wiesbaden, Germany
Tel: 49-611-73650
Homepage: http://www.eirna.com
e-mail: eirna@eirna.com
Director: Georg Neudecker

Montreal, Canada: 514-461-1557

Denmark: EIR - Danmark, Sankt Knuds Vej 11, basement left, DK-1903 Frederiksberg, Denmark. Tel.: +45 35 43 60 40, Fax: +45 35 43 87 57. e-mail: eirdk@hotmail.com.

Mexico City: EIR, Sor Juana Inés de la Cruz 242-2 Col. Agricultura C.P. 11360
Delegación M. Hidalgo, México D.F.
Tel. (5525) 5318-2301
eirmexico@gmail.com

Canada Post Publication Sales Agreement #40683579

Postmaster: Send all address changes to *EIR*, P.O. Box 17390, Washington, D.C. 20041-0390.

Jail This Nazi!

EIR Contents

Correction:
An editing error in the article, "From North Africa to Asia: Making the Deserts Inhabitable," (*EIR*, April 17, 2015, p. 39) mis-stated that "the Vatican has been involved" in the Transaqua Plan for Africa. The plan originated with the engineering firm, Bonifica Spa-IRI-ITALSTAT of Italy, and its former director, Marcello Vichi. The project's first documents were circulated 1982-85. See "Transferring Water from the Congo to Lake Chad: The Transaqua Project," by Dr. Vichi. (*EIR*, July 22, 2011, pp. 31-36).

Science or Fascism

by Benjamin Deniston and Michael Steger

The regular Friday night LaRouchePAC webcast of April 17 featured the life-or-death choice facing mankind, epitomized by the water crisis in California, in presentations by LaRouchePAC Science Team member Benjamin Deniston, and LaRouche Policy Committee member Michael Steger. The moderator is Matthew Ogden. The full webcast can be viewed at https://www. youtube.com/watch?v=_qtfYuJZbGk.

Matthew Ogden: In our webcast tonight, Ben Deniston, who is a relevant expert in this field, will elaborate in detail, will thoroughly discredit, the lies that you are being told by Gov. Jerry Brown and the likes of him, about the so-called water crisis that's happening in the state of California and beyond.

Jerry Brown will insist that the drought is being caused by man-made climate change, or overconsumption of a so-called limited water supply, and is mandating killer cuts in water supply to the people of California. Cuts which will hit the poorest and most vulnerable members of the population first; the people who are already barely surviving at all. The fact is, as Lyndon LaRouche said earlier today, Jerry Brown, and those who agree with him on these matters, are incompetent; and dangerously so. They have no idea what the scientific principle is which drives the global water cycle; and therefore, they have no idea how that water system is to be managed, and how new water supplies can be developed and created.

The problem is not man-made climate change, but the fact that we haven't changed the climate in the way that we should; by mastering and harnessing the physical principles which drive the water cycle as a whole—something that the human species can uniquely do. The fact is, the Earth's water system is not driven primarily by processes here on Earth, but is merely a subordinate feature of a much larger cosmic process on the scale of the Solar System and beyond.

As Mr. LaRouche was saying earlier today, if you look at the implications of the work of Johannes Kepler, who discovered that the Earth is not an isolated body floating in empty space, you see that our planet is an integral part of a much larger system—the Solar System—which is driven by a power which emanates from the Sun, which is itself merely an integral part of a much, much larger galactic system. Then, it's clear that processes here on Earth, including weather systems and the related water cycle, cannot be understood from the standpoint of Earth alone. Anybody who's competent knows that the water system of this planet is controlled by the Solar System, not by the Earth. And anyone who tries to deny that fact, or is making policy based on a contrary view, is dangerously incompetent; because under current conditions, their incompetence will result in the deaths of a large portion of the population of not only California, but the entire United States.

Mr. LaRouche insisted that it must be said that Jerry Brown is on record as an incompetent idiot when it comes to these matters, whose malicious stupidity has disqualified him for public office, and is endangering the lives of the people not only of his state, but of the country as a whole.

The fact is, there are very real solutions that are available and can be implemented with the proper leadership. As we've stressed on previous broadcasts here in recent weeks, this program—which has been elaborated by Ben Deniston—must serve as the basis for a new Presidency of the United States. What my colleague Ben will present to you tonight will thoroughly and irrefutably discredit the lies that you have been given by Jerry Brown. So, I'd like to give the podium to Ben.

FIGURE 1

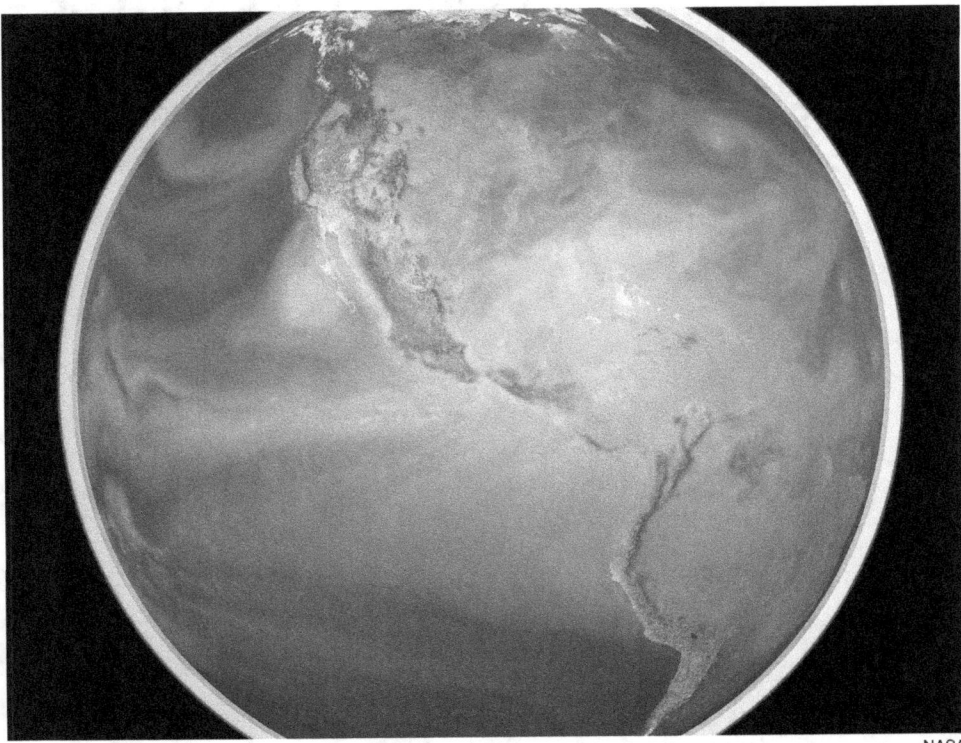

NASA

Atmospheric moisture from the Pacific Ocean spirals up the western coast of North America toward northern Canada and Alaska.

The Water Is There

Benjamin Deniston: Thank you, Matthew. Since you left us with reference to the lies of Jerry Brown, I figured I'd start right there with his first lie that he's promoting all over California, all over the country; which is his claim that the water simply isn't there. This is the situation according to Brown: California has run out of water, the water's not there, it's not available. And Jerry Brown's response to the situation is "Well, deal with it."

Beautiful leadership there—"Deal with it—get used to using less"; that's the leadership of Jerry Brown. And Michael [Steger] is going to get into this just a little bit more, the utter insanity, really degeneration, represented by this Brown governorship. And the fact that this is life or death for many people in California; and Jerry Brown is committing to a depopulation policy for the state by his policies, by his approach to the so-called water crisis.

This is the first lie—he says the water's not there.

Well, the water *is* there; the water's actually all over the place, it just needs to be managed and developed from the right level.

Now, I've got a number of videos and images to take us through the perspective of this higher-level manage-

ment of the water system that we need to start moving towards; that gives mankind a new ability—not just in California, but globally—to handle the water needs for mankind well into the future. As we've said repeatedly, water is not a finite resource. If somebody thinks water is a finite resource, they need to get their head examined.

There is an immense amount of water, and we don't use it up; it exists in cyclical processes that mankind can increasingly manage, improve, develop, and expand. We can create the cycles needed to provide the freshwater supplies, the freshwater systems where they're needed; to provide for the needs of mankind. We can do that. And what we're going to discuss here tonight is the higher perspective that we need to drive towards, which will enable the greatest leaps in mankind's management of the global water system.

So, if we can have the first video (**Figure 1**) displayed on the screen here. We see a very nicely done animation, produced by NASA, on the global moisture system. What you're seeing are the flows of moisture over the oceans, over the land, in a fashion that occurs all the time.

We zoom in on the particular interaction we're con-

FIGURE 2

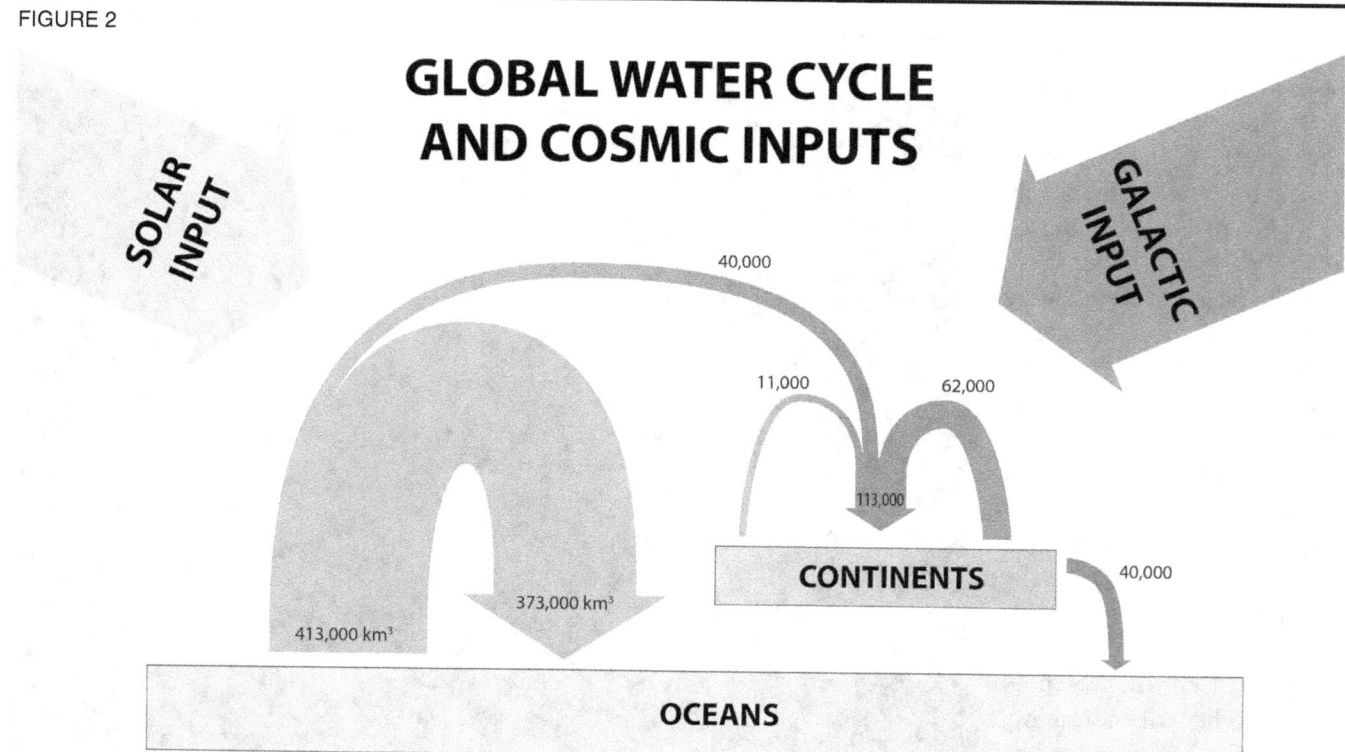

GLOBAL WATER CYCLE AND COSMIC INPUTS

SOLAR INPUT

GALACTIC INPUT

40,000

11,000

62,000

113,000

CONTINENTS

40,000

373,000 km³

413,000 km³

OCEANS

LPAC/Benjamin Deniston

This diagram of the global water cycle shows evaporation of moisture from the oceans, its transfer over land where it precipitates, participates in life, human activity, and interaction with the waters of the continent, before running off back into the ocean. All the flows are given in cubic kilometers of water per year. The cycle is powered and modulated by solar and galactic inputs.

cerned about here: the interaction of the Pacific Ocean with the western half of the North American continent. And, as you can see, there's an immense amount of water flowing throughout the whole system. This atmospheric moisture pattern is really the source of all water supplies on land that people normally think of. When people think of water supplies, they think of rivers, lakes, snowpack, groundwater, etc. But all of these things that people think of as the water supplies, are really an effect generated by these atmospheric moisture flows. The source depositing all the water on the land that we utilize, that we develop, that we depend upon, are these flows of atmospheric moisture. This is the source of what people traditionally think of as the freshwater supplies.

A Shadow of the Cosmos

But what we're going to discuss here tonight. is that mankind does not have to depend solely upon the water that's been deposited on the land. And we can go to this level of these atmospheric systems. But to do that, we have to understand that what we just saw there in that animation, what we talk about when we reference atmospheric water systems, is really a shadow. It's an effect

of certain forces, certain larger processes. And it's mankind uncovering and understanding those larger processes which will give us new tools for understanding how to manage the effects, the shadows, that we experience with the atmospheric moisture system.

Figure 2 is a relatively basic depiction of the global water cycle. Again, as I just referenced, you see the evaporation of ocean water, most of which never makes it on land, but that which does make it on land—you can see that kind of upper curve stretching from the flow from the oceans over the continents. That is the source of all water on land that we tend to deal with, that we utilize, that we have to work with under the existing or old conception of just managing the surface water flows—what gets deposited.

But as you see indicated in this graphic, that process of atmospheric transfer of moisture from the oceans to the land, the source of all of our water supplies that we depend on and utilize, is driven by cosmic factors. It's driven, and managed and modulated by activities that don't come from the Earth; that aren't determined by the Earth, that aren't affected by the Earth, but come from outside the Earth's system.

You have, on the one hand, solar activity which drives the entire process. The evaporation of all the ocean water that becomes the source of all the freshwater in the cycle is done by solar activity. The Sun is evaporating immense amounts of ocean water; desalinating it, purifying it, filling the atmosphere with this atmospheric moisture, which then is the source of the water cycles over land. So, that's driven by solar activity that drives the whole process. That's not an Earth-based process; it's driven by the activity of the Sun, the Solar System.

FIGURE 3

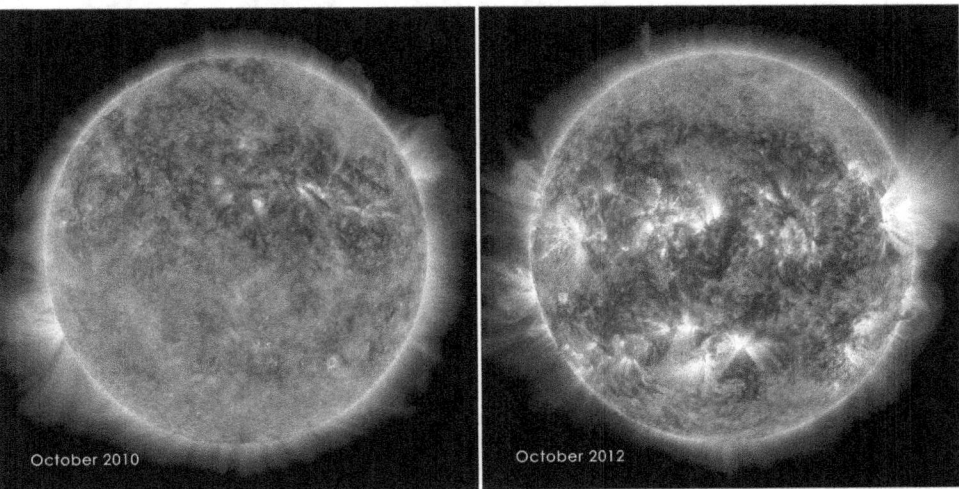

October 2010

October 2012

NASA

These images from NASA's Solar Dynamics Observatory show how varied our Sun can be in its activity. The bright areas seen in the picture from 2012 are areas of increased magnetic flux and other activity on the Sun's surface. Sometimes these erupt into solar flares, which can send charged materials toward the Earth.

So, you have the whole cycle being initiated, created by this cosmic effect, this solar driver.

On the other side, you have the activity of the galaxy more generally, which is constantly at play. We right now, as you're watching this, as I'm speaking to you here, we're being bombarded by the effects of radiation from the galaxy generally. It fills the entire atmosphere; it's a constant input determining certain conditions, certain qualities, of the atmosphere as a whole. And it's these qualities which are affected by this galactic factor, this galactic radiation, which play a major role in affecting when atmospheric moisture condenses from a vapor form to a liquid form and precipitates.

So, again, a cosmic effect constantly coming in, a regular input into the system, playing a critical role in determining the general water cycle that we experience, that we think of—which is really a shadow of the effects of these cosmic processes. So on the one side, in the initiation, you have this solar driver pumping the whole atmosphere full of freshwater; on the other end, you have this galactic, cosmic radiation input affecting the conditions which facilitate when that water falls out of the sky, where it does so, etc.

Climate Change and the Sun

So, when we're talking about the water system, we're not dealing with an Earth-based process; we're dealing with a process which reflects and expresses these inputs from the Sun and beyond the Sun—the galactic system.

With that stated, with that as our baseline, we have to pose the question, "What happens when these cosmic factors change; when they vary; when they fluctuate?" If our climate, our water system, our water cycle, is an expression of these cosmic effects; if the water system of the Earth is an expression of this subsuming activity of the Sun organizing the Solar System as a whole, what happens when the Sun changes?

The second video (**Figure 3**) illustrates what types of variations we know the Sun goes through. We have footage of the Sun from 2010 and 2012, side by side. And you can see right there, there's a significant variation in the amount of activity going on in the Sun. In 2012, there's just generally more activity; more spots that reflect sunspots, magnetic fluxes, variations in activity going on, on the surface of the Sun than in 2010.

Now this should give you an image that the Sun is not just sitting there doing the same thing all the time. It's changing what it does; it cycles every decade. The entire magnetic field of the Sun flips every 11 years; which is an incredible feat, given the size of the Sun. This thing is massive, and it goes through a pole reversal every 11 years; the magnetic field completely flips.

As these 11-year cycles proceed, the Sun varies in its activity. Most significant for the effect we're talking about here is, it varies in its magnetic effects. The mag-

FIGURE 4

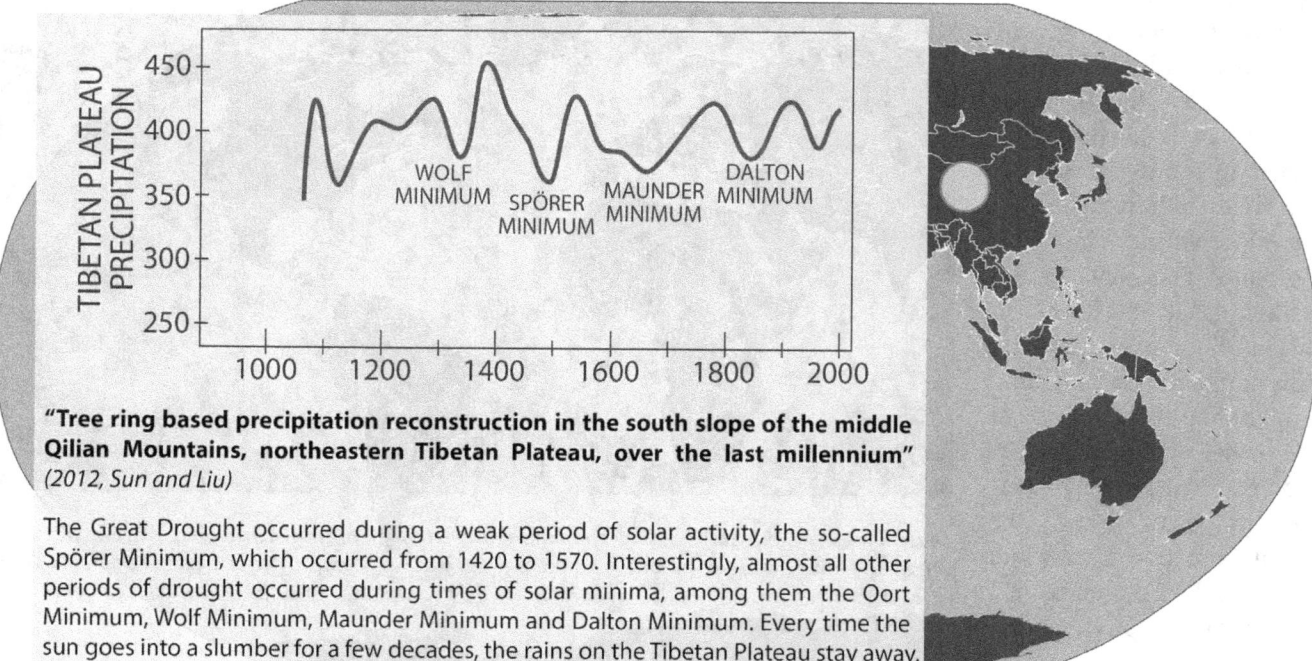

"Tree ring based precipitation reconstruction in the south slope of the middle Qilian Mountains, northeastern Tibetan Plateau, over the last millennium" *(2012, Sun and Liu)*

The Great Drought occurred during a weak period of solar activity, the so-called Spörer Minimum, which occurred from 1420 to 1570. Interestingly, almost all other periods of drought occurred during times of solar minima, among them the Oort Minimum, Wolf Minimum, Maunder Minimum and Dalton Minimum. Every time the sun goes into a slumber for a few decades, the rains on the Tibetan Plateau stay away.

netic field created by the Sun plays a very significant role in modulating the interaction between the radiation coming from the galaxy into the Solar System and what the Sun is doing. This is a factor that is constantly in flux and changing, as the Sun goes through these cycles. What you saw in that video is largely an expression of the changing magnetic activity, the magnetic field of the Sun.

Figure 4 is one depiction of a study showing what types of things happen to our climate system, our water system, our water cycle, when the Sun goes through variations and changes. This is on a timescale of about the past 1,000 years, looking at the variations in precipitation on the Tibet Plateau in China. And we were able to measure the variations in the sizes of tree rings in some very old trees up there, which allowed the scientists to get a sense of how the precipitation, the water flow up there, changed over this past 1,000-year time period.

What they saw in this study was that the amount of water, the amount of precipitation in this particular region, fluctuated. But it fluctuated in direct correspondence to records for how the Sun changed, how the Sun fluctuated. These so-called minimums, indicated here on the graphic, are periods that we've already documented as times of extremely low solar activity; the Dalton minimum, the Maunder minimum some people

might have heard of, the Spore minimum. Based on other records, we have indications that in these times, the Sun got very inactive, very quiet, very relaxed. It took a breather or something; it took some time off. And what we see in these records in the Tibet Plateau, is that when the Sun got weaker; in direct correspondence with that, we saw changes in precipitation, in how the water cycle operated.

That shouldn't be a surprise! The Sun is driving the whole process; the Sun is the bulk input to driving the whole climate system on Earth. So, when we see solar variation, it shouldn't be a surprise that we see changes in climate and in precipitation and in the water cycle.

The Sun as a Driver

Let's go to **Figure 5**. I've just compiled a quick depiction of other locations where similar studies have been done. Obviously, I'm not going to go through all of these, for the sake of time, here, but every one of those locations indicated on the map, is a location where we see records of climate, and activity of the water cycle, in particular, changing and varying, in correspondence with changes in solar activity.

So, this is not some isolated study in one remote part of the world. This is all over the world. Some regions tend to get colder, some regions tend to get drier, some regions even tend to get wetter, when the Sun becomes

FIGURE 5

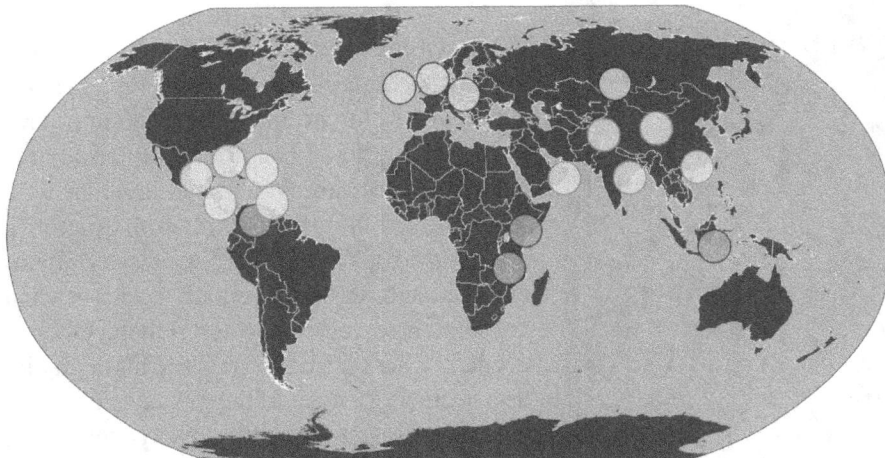

The yellow and blue circles indicate areas where studies have correlated variations in intensity of solar activity with changes in climate, including precipitation.

less active. And, that's just a sampling of a larger array of studies that indicate this. I've just selected these for illustrative purposes, here.

So, the point is, recognizing this solar effect, the role of the Sun as the organizing force in the Solar System, governing and driving the hydrological cycle, the water cycle, on Earth, we now see indications for how, when the Sun goes through cyclical variations and changes, we see corresponding effects back here on Earth.

On the one hand, again, you have the change in the amount of energy output by the Sun itself. But also, you have actually larger changes in the strength of the Sun's magnetic field; it's kind of the governing influence on the Solar System. So, as the Sun gets weaker, the strength of its surrounding sphere of influence gets weaker, and allows a greater effect from inter-stellar space, from the galaxy more generally, to come in and influence systems here on Earth, including the water cycle and the climate system.

So, these are two ways the Sun acts as a direct input into the system, but then also into the water system, and also is a modulating factor, governing and affecting the role of the galactic input into the water system—which, as I referenced in the beginning, is a critical factor determining how and when the water that's in the atmosphere, reaches the right conditions when it can change into a liquid state and precipitate, fall out of the atmosphere, kind of closing the other end of the atmospheric cycles. You have these cosmic

[. . .] boundary conditions on both sides of this atmospheric expression, this atmospheric shadow, in water, of these cosmic effects.

Traveling Through the Galaxy

So, that's an indication of the role of the Sun itself. But we also have a larger scale to look at, too. We have the fact that our Solar System itself experiences different regions of the galaxy, through its motions through the galactic system; that our Solar System is actually orbiting through our galactic system, and experiencing very different environments. The Solar System is moving into and out of large regions of dense clouds of gas and dust. It's moving into and out of these spiral arms of our galaxy. It's moving above and below the disc, the plane of our galactic system. So, it's going through all kinds of stuff, and it's experiencing different environments as it does so, and these have different cosmic radiation effects on the Solar System, and on our Earth, and on our Earth's climate, on our atmospheric system.

If we go to the third video (**Figure 6**), we have a depiction of just one of these motions kind of separated out—just a very simplistic illustration of the motion of our Solar System above, and then moving below, and then heading back above, the plane of our galaxy. Our galaxy is a disc-like structure, relatively thin, compared to its overall size. What we know is that the Solar System tends to move above and below this galactic disc, as it travels through the galaxy.

And now, recent records have indicated that, again, the climate system on Earth changes in correspondence to these different galactic environments. When we're above or below the galactic plane, we tend to get warmer

FIGURE 6

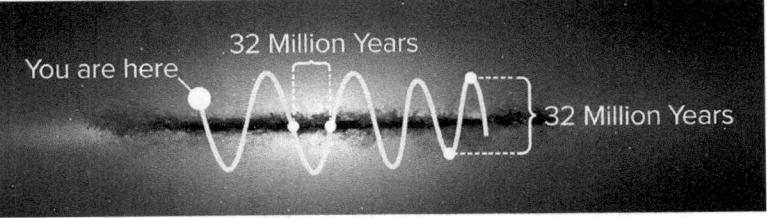

FIGURE 7

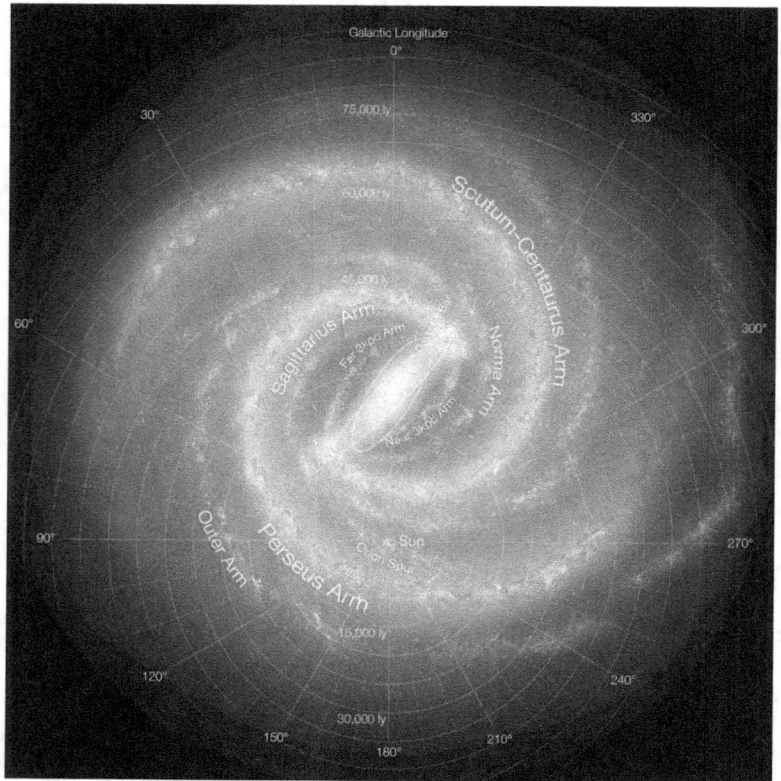

NASA

As our Sun travels through the galaxy, it is believed to move both up and down, rising above and below the galactic disk, and around, passing through the spiral arms (dense regions of ongoing star formation).

galactic environments that our whole Solar System is experiencing.

Now if we go to **Figure 8**, we see that, as we move into and out of the different spiral arms of the galaxy, we see dramatic changes, again, in the climate and the temperature. This is something that's been documented for the past decade or more—that as our Solar System's moved into these spiral arm structures, you tend to get major cooling events, major climate changes. Not even ice ages, but what are sometimes referred to as "global ice-house events," where it's not just a little bit of glaciation occurring. Much of the planet can be covered in ice, in glaciers. Huge events. So, again, these correspond directly to the motions of our Solar System, through the galactic system, through the spiral arms, in particular.

As was stated, we have the water system, and particularly, this atmospheric component of the water system, which is the source of all the water we have on land, and which we depend upon and deal with and manage, up until this point, as being influenced and driven by these cosmic factors, these changes in solar activity, changes in the relationship of the

climates, warmer global climate environments, when we're above or below the galactic plane.

When we're crossing through the middle of the galactic plane, we tend to get cooler environments. The Earth's climate system, the Earth's hydrological system as well, responds to these different galactic environments because, as we stated at the beginning, the hydrological system, the water system, the climate system more generally, are expressions of these cosmic factors. So, we know that when we move above and below the galactic plane, we see indications that the Earth's climate system cools and warms and changes, in correspondence to that.

If we go to the next video (**Figure 7**), we see one other illustration of this, which is the motion of our Solar System kind of orbiting through the galaxy, moving into and out of our galaxy's spiral arms. So, again, different

FIGURE 8

GALACTIC COSMIC RAY FLUX AND TEMPERATURE

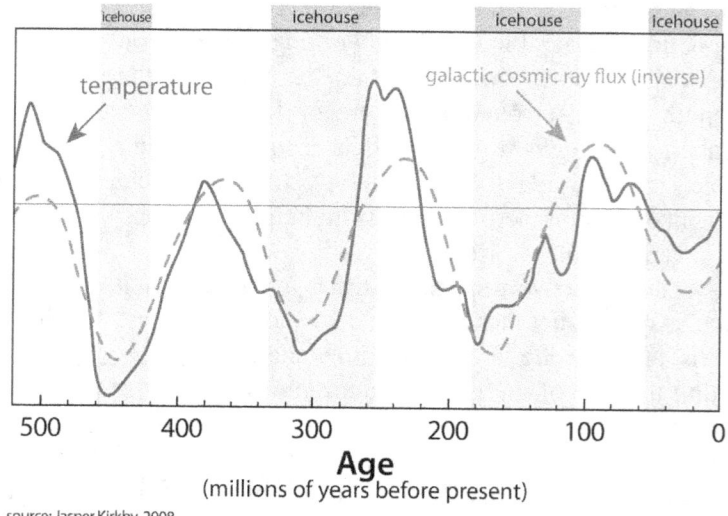

source: Jasper Kirkby, 2008

LPAC

Data from the past 500 million years shows a clear correlation between the flux of galactic cosmic rays into our atmosphere, and changes in global temperature.

Solar System to the galaxy—that our water system, our atmospheric water system, our water cycle, is an expression of these larger cosmic processes. So when these cosmic processes change and vary, we see corresponding changes and fluctuations.

The Cosmic Environment

Now, again, I'll just make a kind of necessary note. Apparently, this is a major surprise to people like Jerry Brown: that the climate, apparently, changes! I guess they never took middle-school geology or geological history classes. But, yes, it's true: the climate on Earth changes. The climate of the Solar System changes. The climate of the galaxy changes. Whether you choose to eat beef, or not; or, whether you choose to drive an SUV, has nothing to do with that. But, the climate does change, and we are affected by these climate changes, as California is now experiencing, largely as an effect of these larger processes.

The point is, we're now at the point where we're beginning to recognize this. The science is coming in, the studies are coming in. We're starting to get a better realization of these cosmic effects, these cosmic driving forces in our water system, in our climate system. That the water cycle that we depend upon, the water cycle that we need to improve and manage for the future of mankind, is not an Earth-based process. It doesn't come from the Earth, it's not driven by the Earth, it's not modulated by what the Earth does.

There are processes on Earth that have effects, sure. Life has effects, geological activity has effects; those are there. But what we're beginning to realize is that the large driving factors, as we just went through, governing global ice ages and global warming, governing variations in weather patterns and precipitation in drought, in flood regions, are associated with these larger-scale solar and related galactic effects, which drive this atmospheric component of the water system, which is more of a shadow, an expression of these larger forces.

So we're beginning to realize this. We're beginning to realize that we live in a cosmic environment. We're

FIGURE 9

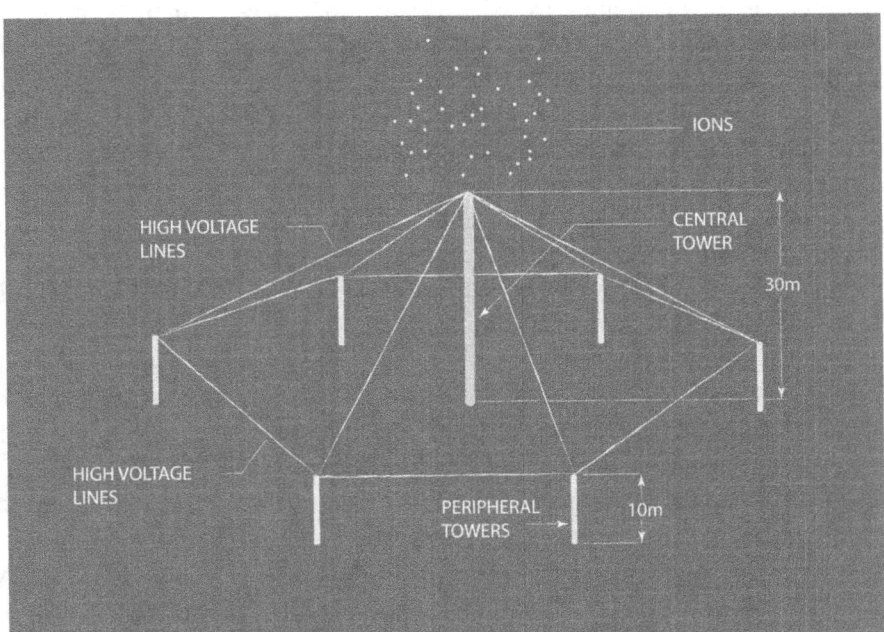

This is a simple schematic of the ELAT system, one of the ionization technologies used to affect the electrical conditions of the atmosphere which contribute to rainfall. Similar systems are currently, or have previously been used across the globe, and have shown promising results in our ability to modulate rainfall in a targeted way.

dependent upon the activity of an environment driven by cosmic processes, solar and galactic processes.

Managing the Water System

The point of all this, is not that we now sit back and say, "OK, that's what it is"; the point is that we, as mankind, then utilize this new knowledge, these new insights, to enable us to improve our ability to manage that system. That's what this is telling us right now, with respect to the crisis in California, in terms of addressing the water needs in California, but throughout the Southwest and throughout the world more broadly. What we're looking at is the perspective on a higher-order understanding of what the system is that we're actually dealing with, that we're actually dependent upon, and then utilizing that higher understanding to change how we can interact with it, to manage it in completely new ways.

And **Figure 9** is the last image, a very simple schematic of some of the technologies that are being developed, which just begin to open the door to how mankind can start to tap into these processes. This is a schematic for a so-called artificial ionization system, of the technology developed in Russia in the 1980s, and utilized for over a decade successfully in Mexico, referred to as ELAT technology, which stands for "electrification of the atmosphere." And through these ionization systems, we've already demonstrated for years now, that mankind can actually manage and modulate these electrical and ionization conditions of the atmospheric system, which are the conditions that play a major role in determining how the atmospheric components of the water cycle operate.

In laymen's terms, we've used these systems to increase precipitation, even to inhibit rainfall where we didn't want it. This has been done; it's being done right now. There are more trials going on. This is a beginning development of a whole perspective of managing these atmospheric conditions of the water cycle to our benefit, to ensure the water goes where it's needed, to ensure that the water doesn't go where it's not needed, to take a higher-order control over the water system, to provide for the water needs of mankind.

So this is one technology, but it's a technology that comes under this broader perspective, of mankind acting and operating on the scale of the Solar System. That really is what we're talking about.

We're talking about mankind moving to the level— not physically, not biologically. More important than that, moving conceptually, mentally, creatively—to the level of the Solar System, understanding that the Earth is subsumed by that, and acting on the Earth systems from the standpoint of acting on the level of the Solar System as a whole. And reaching beyond that, starting to look to the galactic system; that mankind can change his actions on Earth, to be in coherence with mankind's unique ability to understand the Solar System, the galaxy, and how these systems subsume and determine what happens on Earth. Mankind can act on Earth in a unique way, informed by these understandings.

And the effect of that will be, if we were to do it, no water crisis. We can manage the water crisis, if we go to this perspective, if we go to this level.

Morons for Zero Growth

And so, to round this off for my component of the discussion here, I think there's a dramatic irony in this situation we're looking at, because what I'm putting on the table is work that's going on. These are studies that are ongoing, this is research that is happening, that points in a very important and profound direction, that mankind can move to this higher level, and that we can

manage all of our water crises from this higher level and deal with them, by going to this level of the Solar System, so to speak.

And that's something unique to mankind. That's what mankind can do, specifically. This is a new expression of the power of mankind, as a uniquely creative species, different from any animal species on this planet. And with that being the case, this now being demonstrated and developed, we're starting to get a taste of this potential direction, and a greater understanding of what mankind is on this planet, as a creative force that can reach beyond the planet.

In this context, you get Jerry Brown, you get these idiots, who are running around saying, "We've reached the limit to growth. We've realized we reached the limit; that's as much as we can do. You know, we ran out of water. What're you going to do? We just have to kill some people now."

What morons! We're looking at the perspective of mankind completely moving to a new level of understanding of what this water system even is we're dealing with, and then you get *complete idiots* out there, saying, "This is the limit to growth, we can't keeping growing. Mankind's run into his boundary conditions. That's it, we can't go any further."

It would be laughable, if it weren't so criminal. If people's lives weren't dependent upon whether we let Jerry Brown continue his genocide policies or not.

This is idiocy! The guy thinks we've run out of water! The whole planet's covered in water, there's water everywhere. We ran out of smart people, like his father, who knew how to manage it, and we were left with a bunch of idiots like Jerry Brown, who bought into this crazy, '68er depopulation ideology, who are being run by people who want to depopulate the planet.

So we didn't run out of water. We're on the verge of a completely new perspective of mankind's relation to water. But what we need to do is get rid of the idiots holding us back, and getting in our way, and I think that's what Michael is going to get into, so I'll leave it at that.

Ogden: Thank you, Ben. Our next guest tonight is Michael Steger, who is a leading member of the LaRouchePAC Policy Committee, who, as viewers of this website know, participates on a weekly basis in the discussion that we have with Mr. LaRouche on Mondays. He is a former candidate for United States Congress, and is currently leading the fight, on the ground in California.

The Case of California

Michael Steger: Thanks, Matt. What Ben just presented was really a foundation and a basis for a revolution in economic policy, for this nation, and for the world. And because of the dire crisis we're facing in California, which is not simply the drought—the drought is compounding what is the breakdown of the U.S. economy over the last four or five decades. Now in that context, we took Ben's proposal to address the water crisis, which is not only technologies such as nuclear desalination or ionization, but a fundamental shift in how we think of ourselves in the universe and in the Solar System. We took that proposal to Sacramento, thinking there might be some living souls there, willing to consider policies to address the crisis the state now faces.

And this is a *real crisis*. This is a crisis for 38 million people, many of whom are barely, at this point, surviving, and I think that has to be a point made, because the vulnerability of the U.S. population today *cannot* tolerate this kind of stupidity and incompetence from Brown and the other people associated with this policy, which includes the Bush family.

We brought our policy to Sacramento, and it was considered criminal! It was considered a crime to even discuss the idea that the water crisis could be solved; that there was, indeed, no water crisis; that you could, indeed, bring water into the areas of California through the technology, through the policies, and through the research Ben just presented, as he has done in his papers and in the ongoing discussions. And that tells you the kind of fascism that's taking place in Sacramento. And it is not the first time that we've been told that they are not interested in increasing water supply in California: They are interested in "conserving water."

'Brown Is the New Green'

That brings us to the point of Brown and the fascist policy in Sacramento, because this is *not* about conservation. This is not about "we're all in this together" in public conservation. You go back to April 1, when Jerry Brown—and now, there are signs all over California for those of you who haven't made it out here, yet: "Brown Is the New Green." But Jerry Brown gets up on April 1 and says: I'm enforcing a law of a 25% mandatory cut in water. That was going to be mitigated by water agencies with a for-profit motive, so already the idea of public conservation is really just a façade covering the fact of privatization of the water supply of the state.

We've had that happen in California before, as with the public utility for electricity. It was called the "Enron disaster," and it was explicitly targeting the most vulnerable population in California, for record so-called financial profit, while killing the population—and that is fascism. That is what Lyndon LaRouche identified in a debate in 1971, as the fascist policies of people like Milton Friedman, people like Henry Kissinger, people like George Shultz. And George Shultz in California is a factor in this policy.

So you've got this policy now, of pushing water conservation. Now the reality is, 25% across the board is not accurate, and they're trying to say, "We're going to reduce the water of the more affluent areas more than

gov.ca.gov

On April 1, Gov. Jerry Brown dictated a 25% cut in water usage throughout the state. Here, Brown signs a State of Emergency in January calling on state officials to take all necessary actions to prepare for the drought.

the more impoverished areas. We're not going to cut the farmers, we're going to let the farmers have water"—supposedly—"and cut just for the population." And you see the media is painting hysteria, the media like the *New York Times*, which is pushing this no-growth policy. It's the same policy you saw from the rabid neocons that, once the fall of the Soviet Union had happened, history had come to an end, human development and social advancement had ended.

It's not the case. The hysteria is pushed by this fascist policy, by this grouping.

The water agencies are now going to be cutting water in different places. But what you find is that where they're cutting, they have no sense of what's happening on the ground—or, maybe they do. And you have letters written from civil bureaucrats, city employees, people representing certain of the most vulnerable demographics in the state, places like Compton, places like the Central Valley, or Fresno, or Bakersfield. And what they're saying, what they're painting is a very clear picture: that a 20% cut in water will hit people who are already having a hard time paying for rent, or for food, for medical bills, for people who are already not watering their lawns, the so-called—you know, these political terms today: "the low-hanging fruit."

The low-hanging fruit are people like Jerry Brown! Not the so-called green grasses and ornamental landscaping.

But places like Compton, the impoverished cities of California that are not part of the real estate bubble, not part of this Internet bubble, this Wall Street fraud of an economy, are not spending huge amounts of water on these areas. They're limiting their usage of these public utilities towards basic needs and requirements, and that's a helluva lot more than the five gallons that some of these people in the Nestlé Company, and other privatized water companies, want to allocate to the population.

So when you make a 20% cut to people who are already this vulnerable, you're not "nudging" their behavior toward using a little bit less water for their lawns or washing their new cars. You're saying, "You're going to bathe less. You're going to be less sanitary, in an area which is going to have the propagation of more diseases." You're going to be giving a clear message: "You're not wanted." And the prices of water are going to be increasing under this regimen, until the population is eradicated, because as Jerry Brown referenced, California only supported 400,000 people for a very long time.

And if that's the case, Jerry, well, you should start with yourself, and we can get on with development of the water resources of our state and of our nation.

So this is the fascist policy which is laid out in California.

Pitting Farmers Against Eaters

The same is true for the farmers: For three years, farmers have already had their water cut. The state program is allocating a very small percentage. The Federal program built by Franklin Roosevelt has been allocating zero now, for two years, or will be.

So the farmers have already taken major measures, and the farmers produce something which is not a new app for your smartphone; it is not an inflated price for real estate; they're producing the food and the nutrition, for not only California and the nation, but also globally.

So you have this media hysteria pitting these two groups against each other. And as even the farm leaders in the state have said: When we meet with the governor, we have the farm groups; then you have the environmentalist groups. You don't have people representing areas of the urban population, the poor parts of California. They aren't at the table.

Are they concerned about the farmers using water for food? I don't think they're concerned about the farmers using water for food; I think they'd like to make sure the farmers have enough water to produce enough food, so there's enough for them! That the prices are within their budget, that they can afford to feed their families. That's probably what's going to be their concern, not what the environmentalists are putting out as a concern.

And there is no concern for the Delta smelt, there is no concern for environmental concerns—these environmentalists have done more to pollute the environment than any other part of the U.S. population! They are the ones destroying the environment, hands down! They're the ones polluting the oceans, because they restricted the science and the technology to deal with the actual reality that it's *good* for mankind to develop; it's *good* for populations to grow, and you need to sustain and develop that technology to make that possible. So we should get rid of the environmentalists if we want to clean up the environment. And we should start with Jerry Brown.

What Jerry Brown has done, then, with this policy, this so-called water conservation, this cloak of public "conservation," which is really the privatization of water, is a crime. It's a crime to the state Constitution, where water itself is identified as part of the general welfare of the state, because of the arid condition of the state, which is probably what makes it such a good growing area; this is part of the state Constitution.

And on this basis alone, Jerry Brown is criminal, and his remaining in office is a crime! This *is* a fascist program, it *is* Hitler-like policies! "You have an economic problem? Reduce the population and target the most vulnerable." We've had a squad of four individuals and organizers in the Central Valley for the last few days, and the people who are targeted by these policies, for their livelihood, for their contribution to the nation and to society, know what's happening: that this is existential and it is life-or-death.

Send the Nazis to Jail!

And the point now is not just to leave it there, but to recognize the actions that must be taken. Brown must go, out of office, into jail, prosecuted, along with people like Dennis O'Connor, and the rabid ideologues of Sacramento; and what Ben just laid out must become the policy for the state and for the nation.

Now, the bigger question is where this came from. Because this is not just happening in California, but California has been a test case, not only under the Brown program for water, but look at the program we've had now, four years of Jerry Brown's policies, added onto the eight years of his policies in the 1960s and '70s, which is what shut down the nuclear power program, not just in California, but across the country. That same nuclear power which could be providing desalination capabilities today.

But you also had Arnold Schwarzenegger for seven years, and you had the Enron program for three years before that: a direct policy continuity from George Shultz, a direct policy of the fascists who put in Pinochet in Chile. The same type of fascism, that you see promoted by Obama today in Ukraine; the same kind of Nazis that Obama's promoting in Ukraine are now dominating and have been dominating Sacramento policy for up to 15 years. And it's not the Republicans who are going to solve the problem, because they bought this hook, line, and sinker with Bush and Cheney, *and* with Schwarzenegger.

A New American Presidency

And what we have to do today, then, is to define a new American Presidency, independent of both this Republican grouping who are out to kill us, clearly, and of this rabid environmentalist, pro-drug policy of the likes of Shultz, or Jerry Brown, who clearly have a depopulation agenda. This is the criminality that has been tolerated by the American people for far too long. And it is happening in the United States, it's happening in California as a test case. It's the same policy you see in Ukraine, and it's the same policy you see in Greece today.

What Ben has presented is a scientific orientation of development and technology. And that's what the BRICS nations are responding to, this kind of fascist economic program, which was warned about by Mr. LaRouche in the 1960s and '70s. And either we fight today to end it, or we're not going to exist much longer.

And that is very clear in the case of California and its people.

Obama's Fascist Onslaught

by Nancy Spannaus

April 21—In his drive for fascist dictatorship and war, Adolf Hitler knew he had to remove any roadblock that could be raised by the parliament. Using the hoked-up Reichstag Fire fraud, Hitler rammed through his Enabling Act which permitted him, in the name of the "emergency," to make the laws himself. Once that authority was ceded "temporarily," the die was cast.

Barack Obama is taking a page from Hitler's book with his current drive for "Fast Track" authority for his secretive Trans-Pacific Partnership (TPP) free-trade deal.

What Obama wants to sign is no partnership, but yet another of his attempted direct attacks on the growing economy of China. Otherwise, the deal is being kept hidden, because it is also an attack on the United States economy and people.

Should he succeed in ramming through such Fast Track authority, Obama will be enabled to enact a largely *classified, top-secret* agreement on trade that will rip up U.S. laws and those of other sovereign nations in the interests of the fascist financiers dominating Wall Street. Fast Track means Congress will be sidelined, never seeing the deal until it's done—and a major step will be taken toward British puppet Obama's planned war in the Pacific—specifically, against China.

Put simply, "Fast Track" is Obama's chosen path toward consolidation of a global Wall Street-City of London dictatorship, and toward World War III. To stop it, he must be removed constitutionally from power.

The TPP Monster

Negotiations for the TPP have been going on among 12 nations bordering the Pacific Ocean for a number of years. According to Lori Wallach, Public Citizen Global Trade Watch director, the agreement has largely been

Martin O'Malley President in 2016 facebook page

Fast Track "is a race to the bottom, a chasing of lower wages abroad."—Martin O'Malley, April 20, 2015

drafted. It was the intent of the Obama Administration to ram through the legislation in 2014—until heavy opposition from the Democratic leadership in the House and Senate, including then-Majority Leader Harry Reid, led to it being pulled from the agenda.

Democrats, labor unions, and many civic groups are not buying the Obama Administration's argument that "this time" the free-trade deal will not lead to the outsourcing of millions of American jobs, as American workers are forced to "compete" with workers in countries, such as Vietnam, making 60 cents an hour.

"It is a race to the bottom, a chasing of lower wages abroad," charged Democratic Party Presidential pre-candidate Martin O'Malley in an interview with NPR April 20. "And I am appalled by the notion that we're not allowed, as Americans, to read this agreement before our so-called representative institution of the Congress votes on it."

Indeed, until Wikileaks provided the Investment Chapter of the agreement to the *New York Times* in early March, the opponents of the bill didn't know the half of it. *Again, the content of the TPP is being negotiated in secret.*

Specifically, according to the text provided by Wikileaks, the TPP has 29 secret clauses, which are not to be revealed until *four years* after either the agreement is signed, or the negotiations fail! That means, of course, that, even if Congress got a chance to read and debate and vote on the bill, *as the U.S. Constitution provides,* the Members would be deprived of the content of a vast portion of the bill.

According to Wallach, only five of those secret provisions even deal with trade. The most notorious of them known at this time, is the one which establishes the Investor-State Dispute Resolution System, a "corporate tribunal" which would permit any foreign investor from a TPP country to drag the United States, or any other country, before an international tribunal of three corporate attorneys, who would determine if U.S. laws were violating the terms of the treaty. If these corporate attorneys so determined, the U.S. laws (for example, a restored Glass-Steagall Act) would be thrown out! There would be no appeal from the decision of this tribunal, which could *override* the laws (i.e., sovereignty) of any nation or state, for the benefit of the corporate interests involved.

Wallach, in an interview with CSPAN's Washington Journal April 20, asserted that this provision would allow the enforcement of provisions that would override U.S. patent and copyright laws, undermine the negotiated prices for medications under Medicare and other government medical programs, and roll back those financial reforms that have been passed. Other protections for U.S. (or other national) workers could also be nullified, such as preferences for jobs to go to Americans.

Taking Congress's Powers

Even though many of these provisions, permitting corporations to rip up legal protections for U.S. workers and industry, are being kept secret, Obama and his Wall Street backers are well aware that "free trade" does not sit well with the American population. Thus, the drive for Fast Track.

The Fast Track law, first enacted under President Richard Nixon, pulls Congress's Constitutional author-

http://www.aflcio.org

Rally in Washington, D.C., April 20

ity over trade agreements, substituting Executive power. Congress basically gives the President the ability to negotiate the agreement—without any Congressional involvement—to write the implementing legislation, and then hand it over to the Congress for an up or down vote, within 90 days. Only 20 hours of debate are permitted under Fast Track authority; no amendments to the legislation are permitted.

In short, the President—acting on behalf of Wall Street—has dictatorial powers.

It is for this reason that Democrats, in particular, are up in arms against Obama's push to get Fast Track authority for the TPP. Only by relying on the Republicans in the Senate, was Obama able to get a bill drafted that will be heard in the Senate Finance Committee on April 23—a move the would-be dictator hopes will begin a rapid dash for passage in both Houses.

While House Democrats have been mobilizing intensively against the deal for months, recent statements from prominent Senate Democrats—such as New York's Chuck Schumer—suggest that the drive for Fast Track may have problems in the Senate as well. "I don't believe in these agreements any more," said Schumer on April 16. "I've changed."

Although Schumer went on to say that he might eventually support the trade deal, if it passed along with legislation that would allow a crackdown on alleged currency manipulation, he seemed to be strongly against Fast Track. Pressure from within his own state is also growing, as shown by an attack on the Fast Track authority published April 19 in *Politico* by New York State Attorney General Eric Schneiderman. The use of the new tribunals exposed by Wikileaks would "allow large multinational corporations to sue a signatory country for actions taken by its federal, state or local elected or appointed officials that the foreign corporation claims hurt its bottom line," he said.

Schneiderman warned members of Congress from New York to take note. "This should give pause to all members of Congress, who will soon be asked to vote on fast-track negotiating authority to close the agreement," he said. "But it is particularly worrisome to those of us in states, such as New York, with robust laws that protect the public welfare."

Free Trade = New Auschwitzes

April 21—Barack Obama's attempt to steamroll Congress into giving him Fast Track authority is another example of him following the trail of Bush Family fascism. George H.W. Bush devised the "free trade" pact called NAFTA in 1990—a pact finally pushed through in 1992—as a service to his Wall Street/City of London backers. The expanded TPP pact would do the same on a much larger scale.

Lyndon LaRouche denounced the NAFTA free-trade policy as intending to create an "Auschwitz below the border." That it has done, not only by its sanctioning of slave-labor *maquiladora* operations, but by mandating the destruction of agriculture by phasing out tariffs. Mexico is now a nation desperate for the food it can no longer produce, bereft of modern infrastructure, unprotected from financial, drug, and corporate predators.

Devastation has also been wreaked by NAFTA on the U.S. side of the border. The Economic Policy Institute estimates 700,000 jobs lost to runaway shops in Mexico, but even more widespread was the impact driving down wages and benefits in the United States, as employers used the threat of outsourcing to cow workers into submission.

Meanwhile, both the labor unions and a large contingent of Democratic Congressmen are rallying to stop the drive for Fast Track and the TPP. Two large rallies have been held in Washington over the last week, featuring spirited attacks from Sen. Elizabeth Warren (D-Mass.) and others. AFL-CIO President Richard Trumka has vowed that his organization will pull funding from any Congressman who supports the atrocity. The horrors brought on by NAFTA are a living reality to the now-decimated labor movement (see box).

War on China

Beyond the assault on the general welfare of the American population and the U.S. Constitution, in the interests of Wall Street, Obama has another target in mind—China.

From the outset, the TPP was conceived as a means of economic warfare against China, which has been specifically excluded as a potential negotiating partner in the agreement. This contrasts sharply with the Chinese open-ended approach to trade deals, which won the support of the APEC nations last November over Obama's TPP.

Obama's hostile intent toward China—already evident in the militarization of the Pacific with the "Asia pivot"—was open for all to see in his State of the Union this year, when he declared that the U.S. would not let China "write the rules" for trade. In his current push to get Fast Track authority, he has reiterated that attack on China.

But China's approach, as evidenced by its recent long-term trade agreement with South Korea, focuses on the reciprocal lowering of trade barriers and supply bottlenecks over a long period, to actually increase trade and production in each nation. It does not involve granting multinational banks and corporations power over nations.

Obama's outlook not only directly contradicts the Chinese approach, but is part of the pattern of economic warfare that has characterized this Wall Street-owned President. As he did with his attempted sabotage of the Asian Infrastructure Investment Bank, Obama is determined to smash the process of global cooperation being carried out by the BRICS nations, a process in which China is playing the leading role.

There is no negotiating with this President, who is in the pocket of Wall Street and the City. As long as he remains in power, no one is safe.

The French Resistance: A Dialogue With Jacques Cheminade

by Tony Papert

April 21—Jacques Cheminade, born 1941, is a long-time political leader of France, and was twice a candidate for the French Presidency. Jacques is the chairman of Solidarity and Progress, the French sister-organization of the Lyndon LaRouche-allied organizations of the United States and other countries. *EIR*'s Tony Papert interviewed him for 40 minutes on April 17. The transcript has been extensively edited.

EIR: Jacques, last week, Lyndon LaRouche called on Americans to fight a Nazi takeover by the likes of California Governor Jerry Brown. This has forced many of us to look back at the French Resistance of the World War II years, because the Resistance had to fight not only the German occupiers, but also a native French fascist government and its supporters. Can you tell us about your family's relations, and your own over the years, to the wartime Resistance?

Cheminade: Well, my family,—it is saying too much, to say that it was involved in the Resistance. My family was involved in this historical moment when things were extremely ambiguous—and you had to locate in yourself what it really meant to be human, in this period. And my family tried to be human.

The only thing I can mention, which I think is significant for an American audience—I had a cousin of mine, a farmer, a simple farmer, who was arrested and held in a stadium in central France, when the French soldiers were captured. And he told the other prisoners: "Look, this stadium is not very well guarded; it's not closely watched, so we should simply escape!" But only two others agreed to escape with him,—to follow him. Even though, in his own words, it was not so difficult.

EIR: I fear to think what happened to the others.

Cheminade: So, at this point, the issue is that of willful submission, what a French writer, La Boétie, called willful submission: Either you submit, or you decide to fight. And then, if you don't decide to fight, the freedom of the inner self is destroyed. And I think

Julien Lemaître

Jacques Cheminade in Paris, November 2013

that this is the issue of the Resistance, and that we have been carrying this conception in our family,—that there *is* a future, and that it can only be outside the rule of the oligarchy.

EIR: Yes! And Lyndon LaRouche, as you know, has said in the past week, that none of us knows what proportion, what percentage of Americans will fight a Nazi takeover by the likes of Jerry Brown and most of the Republicans; no one knows what proportion will actually fight and what proportion will concede, temporize, negotiate, and ultimately compromise,—and themselves become compromised and destroyed. To me, this reflects the same ambiguity, the same uncertainty in the Resistance.

Cheminade: Well, you never know what other people will do, and you should not care about their opinion. You should never act on the basis of public opinion. If you act on the basis of public opinion, your inner soul is doomed. Enthusiasm for the truth, enthusiasm for the future of humanity, should be what moves you, and that is what is called in the Greek tradition, "the inner god."

EIR: "Enthusiasm," the inner god. Yes.

Cheminade: Inner god—and you should decide there are things you would never do, but much more than that: you should decide there are things that you have to do, and you do these things, and then you see what happens: You inspire people. At the beginning, there are not too many, but at some moment, you have behaved like a human being, and others see your example, and follow your example. And I think that humanity is more contagious than evil is.

EIR: Exactly.

The Inner Source of Resistance

Cheminade: After the fall of France, the population, the majority of the population was not fascist: they were lost,—they were at a loss,—because the people who were in power positions, went over to the wrong side. The population knew that there was something wrong with the elite's going over to the wrong side, but they didn't know what to do, because they had no leaders. And it was then that the voice of Charles de Gaulle was heard. But it was heard only incrementally,—it took many repetitions. You have to understand how most people were shell-shocked by the collapse of the Republic and its Army.

Resistance fighter Marie-Madeleine Fourcade

Marie-Madeleine Fourcade, my late friend from the Resistance, told me that before the Nazi invasion of southern France, on Nov. 11, 1942, there were probably no more than 2,000 people in the whole Resistance. It was a very small body of people who were actually fighting for France.

In the population, some of the French,—or a lot of the French,—behaved, let's say, morally, and saved a lot of children,—Jewish children, or adults,—from their own government, and this is what Serge Klarsfeld had to recognize. He said this happened.

But what was really the most revealing thing, was this collapse of the elite, because the elites were already rotten from the inside, and some of them, as Marc Bloch said,—writing during the war,—had preferred treason. The collapse of France in 1940, was a mixture of treason and incompetence. People in the Army, the old

nobles in the Army, and people in political power, except for a few,—were all ready to submit to fascism, because in their hearts, culturally, they were on that side already. And that's the consequence of the fact that the very ideology of fascism itself, originated in France. These rotten elites hated the Republic, and they hated their own people. For them, as Charles Maurras said, the Nazi invasion was a "divine surprise."

EIR: Now, Lyndon LaRouche has said there must be no compromise, and no negotiation with Nazis. For me, this brings to mind the great Resistance heroes, like the Marc Bloch whom you named, and who was shot by the Nazis; and Marie-Madeleine Fourcade, whom you had the privilege to know personally. And even more so, Charles de Gaulle.

Cheminade: It comes from the heart. You see, in Munich, for example, these people of the White Rose, these youth were in the belly of the beast, and in the very belly of the beast they had the courage to stand up. In France, you had the Missak Manouchian group, called the Immigrant Workforce Movement (MOI),— immigrants who understood the idea of France better than most native Frenchmen.

So, this is a moment which absolutely changes life, and changes other people's lives. And why do you do it? Why do you do it? This is the key thing to ask yourself. You do it because you start to do it, I think, in a way ... and then, you cannot go back. Because if you go back, you appear in your own eyes as a swine,—so you are in the fight.

And I think this is what's very interesting in some people I knew, like Lucie and Raymond Aubrac, who were on the extreme left of the Resistance; and Charles Paperon, who is a friend of ours, a very close friend of ours. He's in his late eighties, and he's one of the prominent persons who was in the Resistance. Others as well.

EIR: The other thing I wanted to raise with you, is the French origin of fascism. We've actually been discussing that here already, and you've just raised it again yourself. Could you talk about that?

Cheminade: Yes. I wrote a preface to Jean Jaurès' book *De la Réalite du Monde Sensible* ["On the Reality of the World of the Senses"], on this issue. Because if you look at the two people who stood up against these fascist roots, there was Jaurès in 1914, when fascism did not exist as a name—but it existed as a concept, as an ideology; and de Gaulle, of course, in 1940, and the people around them. I have long fought to understand exactly how and at what moment, they decided to break completely with that environment, because they had a higher idea of man.

You deserve a very, very long answer on this issue.

EIR: If you would agree to give it, I'd be very happy to hear it.

Fascism's Origins in France

Cheminade: French fascism stems from the French oligarchy. It's obviously not from the French people, and it's not France,—but it's the French oligarchy. Therefore, to understand it, you have to look at it historically,—and the best thing I know of, except for what we ourselves have written on it, is the writing of Simone Weil. I don't know if you're familiar with her. She was a Jew who converted to Christianity, who was a Platonist, and who was in London with de Gaulle during the war. In 1940-1941, she wrote a book, *Some Reflections on the Origin of Hitlerism*, where she reviewed the Roman roots of Hitlerism, and how these Roman roots were principally embodied or assumed in France, through the oligarchy. First it was in Spain, with the tyrannies of Charles V and Philip II—Philip II of the Schiller play *Don Carlos*.

Then it came to France as the absolute monarchy, with Richelieu first, and then Louis XIV. And she mentioned the looting and the murder of the Palatine Wars and the Dutch Wars, which Lyn also discusses. So, we have Louis XIV, and then Napoleon I. And Napoleon I is the key: Napoleon III is the nephew of Napoleon I, but Napoleon I is the key. Because, you have first the reaction to the French Revolution,—because the Revolution was miscarried around the issue of how you eliminate the enemy. It was a kind of Carl Schmitt-syndrome inside the French Revolution: friend versus enemy: you eliminate the enemy, but there is no way to *change* the enemy or the adversary. You have to kill him. So, this inspired Napoleon, who in turn terrorized the whole world. And, again in turn, this Caesarism of Napoleon I justified the restoration of the *ancien*

Jean Jaurès

régime of oligarchical control.

So it's very interesting if you look at Joseph de Maistre. Joseph de Maistre was not really French. He was from Savoy; he was the ambassador of Savoy to Moscow,—but he inspired, of course, the French ideology. He's what we have elaborated: the executioner and the victim. He says that it is necessary, and indeed good, to have an executioner to spread fear. In that sense, the British used and manipulated Napoleon, who was allegedly their enemy, to instill fear and destroy the Continent,—destroying the potential opposition to London, which took over after Napoleon's fall.

The idea of terror and Caesarism, is actually to decompose, to rot the soul of your adversary, so that he loses all energy and submits.

EIR: Exactly!

Cheminade: That's the ideology of fascism, and there were many, many elaborations of that in France. The first was Joseph Arthur de Gobineau, who, in 1855 under Napoleon III, wrote an essay on the inequality of human races. Then Georges Vacher de Lapouge, also in the 19th Century, wrote *The Aryan: His Social Role* [*L'Aryen: Son Rôle Social*]. He says that "there is no such thing as human rights, any more than there are rights for the three-striped armadillo or the syndactile gibbon. ... The very idea of law is a fiction. ... There are only forces,—might; life only maintains itself through death. To live you have to eat, to kill—to kill to be able to eat."

Then, worse, there was Maurice Barrès. He was inspired by Johann Gottfried von Herder, the German forefather of the romantic oligarchical movement. For him, biological determinism is what determines the fate of humanity, and he has a concept of an organicist State. He says that what has to be eliminated is the republicans, the democrats, and the Semites, because they are foreign organs. He promotes "the soil and the dead," which is the same thing as the German *Blut und Boden*. He said, for example, during the Dreyfus Affair, "I know from his racial origins that he is doomed to be a traitor."

In a sense, these fascists define what happened in World War I, with the brutalization, the barbarization of the trenches.

More important, you have Georges Sorel, who

Cheminade and Charles Paperon, co-chair of the Association of Resistance Veterans, at a November 2013 conference of Solidarité & Progrès.

EIRNS/Julien Lemaître

wrote about regenerative violence. So if you put all of that together, you have the famous quote of Charles Maurras from 1931-1933, which is not so well known; he says, in his *Political and Critical Dictionary*: "Socialism, if purged of the cosmopolitan and democratic element, can fit nicely with nationalism, as a well-made glove would fit a beautiful hand." There you have it: national socialism. And this is '31-'33. So you have all of this bad smell, coming from these people who represent a basis for what has happened in the 20th Century.

Another aspect of what I see now in Europe, even in France and Germany, is the smell of Drieu La Rochelle, who committed suicide in 1944 because he had gone with the Nazis. He wrote, "There is the elating, exciting night, where there are no more ideas or opinions, but only feelings."

To that, Charles de Gaulle counterposed that France is an idea,—not so much a territory or a people, but an idea. And de Gaulle also had a sense of who the enemy was. But he said the nation is an idea, and that it only has a true meaning if it serves the cause of humanity, and the commitment to progress,—this he said in his speech at the University of Mexico in 1964. So you have this opposition in France, and you have this clash. On one side, the Synarchists. The basis for the Synarchy, is that you put together a group of people who represent this ideology, and these people can be trusted more than a tyrant, because the tyrant can be either killed or changed. But in an oligarchical

Raymond Aron, head of the Congress of Cultural Freedom

Synarchy, if one man dies, he is replaced by another member of the Synarchy. And on the other side, you have the Republic: freedom, equality, and fraternity—the love for humanity as a power to improve the universe, to make the world better.

EIR: Synarchy: yes—that's exactly what the word means, actually. It's like the Board of Ephors of ancient Sparta.

Cheminade: That was a relatively long answer, but I think it has to be understood. Because if it's not understood, people here tend to say, "Oh, the French fascists,—oh no, I am not a fascist," and so on. In France, people say, "Oh, no, no. Pétain was not exactly a fascist—he was a Franquist. He was more on the side of Franco." So what I say is, "Well, ahem: A Franquist is a fascist more or less stained by the Catholic Church, a Catholic Church soiled by Rome and Aristotle."

EIR: Yes, exactly.

The Executioners of Culture

Cheminade: But there's another point: people don't usually understand how that fits with the British Empire. And you have a very good example of how that fits: It's Raymond Aron. Raymond Aron pretended to be a liberal anti-Communist, but also anti-fascist. And people say that Raymond Aron was right against Jean-Paul Sartre. Well, the truth is that they were both very, very wrong! But Raymond Aron was the head of the Congress for Cultural Freedom (CCF). And he promoted his good friend Bertrand de Jouvenel, who before the war had interviewed Hitler and spread his venom into France! So there you have the link between pre-war fascists and postwar Anglo-American Atlanticists.

EIR: Yes,—the CCF had an unlimited budget, from the CIA, and the Ford and Rockefeller Foundations, to destroy Classical culture, whether in music, painting, or literature,—in favor of modernist crap. This is exactly what you said earlier about rotting-out the mind of the adversary. Of course, it begs the question: who exactly is the adversary here?

"Jaurès and de Gaulle ... with their friends and followers, are what saved our honor as a nation and as a Republic."— Cheminade. De Gaulle is shown here in Britain, 1943.

Cheminade: Exactly. Exactly. There is the book *Who Paid the Piper? The CIA and the Cultural Cold War* by Frances Stonor Saunders, which is also very interesting if you think about France.

In fact, there was a book written in France before that, on the Congress for Cultural Freedom,—denouncing the Congress for Cultural Freedom,—but the oligarchy managed to put this message under the rug, and it was never discussed. So you see the connection between the Congress for Cultural Freedom, and the former Hitler apologists who came back and said, "well, we're innocent: we didn't know where it was all heading." But, they promoted just the same thing after the war, under the cover of anti-communist liberalism,—the same oligarchical ideology under a new mask.

EIR: Typical of what the CCF promoted, is the Stravinsky-Diaghilev ballet *The Rite of Spring*—even if it was first performed decades earlier.

But tell me,—just exactly what *is* the "Rite of Spring?" Why, it's a human sacrifice! Precisely what the looniest of the French Synarchists dabbled in!

Cheminade: Yes,—human sacrifice is interesting in terms of "art," so-called. Because you had all these people, who became absolutely demoralized—because in the 20th Century, they had nothing more to say,—because they were not able to have a sense of the creative, as the most immediate, creative process in the human mind. So, because they had nothing to say, they decided to enjoy destruction—the destruction of art. And finally, the destruction of themselves:

That's why so many committed suicide.

I was reading an author, once very famous in France, who is becoming very famous again: Stefan Zweig,—but he's terrible! It's just awful,—and he also committed suicide in 1942. So if you look at the context of the death of Hitler, it's all a suicidal thrust. Zweig was an anti-Nazi, but yet, still trapped in the same pessimistic, self-destructive obsession.

EIR: And also Obama, to mention a contemporary figure.

Cheminade: He doesn't know it, but he's his own worst enemy! [laughter] He could have been a human being, probably.

EIR: Perhaps,—if he had only made a wiser choice of a mother! Back in Roman times, the Emperor Nero made exactly the same mistake.

Do you have anything more to say to Americans who are confronted by the rise of Nazism within their own country, and don't know much about it?

Cheminade: The other thing, before I close up: If in moments of history like our moment,—or that moment of the Resistance,—if you stay in the gray zone, you become a collaborator, what we called a "*collabo*" in the French Resistance. And then you become a fascist.

EIR: Exactly, that's the point.

Cheminade: Because you see your oppression as a destiny, and you turn against the others, and then against yourself in the end. You become your own Executioner, the Executioner of your humanity.

EIR: Yes, you're absolutely right. And this goes to what Lyndon LaRouche has been referencing exactly in this connection. Namely: those who compromise and, as a result, are themselves compromised by their compromise, and also corrupted and destroyed by that slogan of: "Be practical!"

Cheminade: Yes. If you were practical in 1940, you made a lot of money in the stock market, because the French stock market went up tremendously, in 1940 and '41. Because there were these connections to German military production, and then, also, there was the Atlantic Wall. French firms made a lot of money with the Atlantic Wall. [laughs]

EIR: That's fascinating.

Cheminade: The last thing I would say is: "Never stay in the gray zone. Think about your capacity to become a human, as Jaurès, de Gaulle and others did." I mention Jaurès and de Gaulle in France, because they are, with their friends and followers, what saved our honor as a nation and as a Republic.

Zeus versus Prometheus in California

by Michael Steger and Paul Gallagher

April 18—What is now hitting California will, as often before, hit the rest of the country next. An austerity policy of severe, mandated cuts in water supply by Gov. Jerry Brown, combined with escalating water prices leading toward Enron-style privatization, is being watched by numerous other states with water emergencies throughout the West. It is a fascist economic policy, hitting hardest at poor communities in California which cannot further reduce water use without depopulating, and farmers having to give up their livelihood. This is a population-reduction policy, being enforced by Brown's and his advisors' insistence that there is no way to increase water supplies to California.

California's green fascist governor Jerry Brown stopped the development of nuclear power in the state during his first two terms in that office in the 1975-1983 period, says veteran LaRouche Democratic political leader in the state, Harley Schlanger. In doing so, Brown guaranteed that a future western dry cycle would become a severe drought in the nation's most productive state—a drought in which the recycled Brown is now imposing water cuts which will, and are intended to, reduce the population.

"He ran a radical environmentalist policy against nuclear power, against the development of resources in the state, and at the same time an austerity policy," says Schlanger. Without nuclear, California lacks one of the key immediate means of using the vast Pacific lapping at its 800-mile coast to produce freshwater in quantity for the parched state. It will take five years to create that capacity now, and that will take removing Brown from office immediately; he is as much an anti-nuclear diehard as ever. He also recently blurted out that he thinks the stable population capacity over the very long term has been 300-400,000, just 1% of its current population. "The recycling of Jerry Brown is a radical environmentalism which is committed to population reduction," Schlanger says. "His is a Nazi policy."

EIRNS/Chris Jadatz

Harley Schlanger has been a political leader and opposition activist in California for more than two decades. "What we've done, with the organizing we've done against Schwarzenegger, and what we did earlier against Jerry Brown in the 1980s," Schlanger says, "is that we've defined the issue, as being man as a creator, innovator, as someone who can advance nature for the benefit of human society, versus those who say that to do that, destroys Mother Nature."

California has at many times, and in many fields, been the national leader in the application of science and technology, of human creativity, to the problems of economy and production. In the time of FDR's Presidency and then the governorship of Edmund "Pat" Brown (1959-67)—Jerry Brown's father—California was the center of, effectively, a second American Revolution in agriculture, industry, and economic infrastructure, making it alone one-sixth of the United States economy.

"What we've done, with the organizing we've done against Schwarzenegger, and what we did earlier against Jerry Brown in the 1980s," Schlanger says, "is that we've defined the issue, as being man as a creator, innovator, as someone who can advance nature for the benefit of human society, versus those who say that to do that, destroys Mother Nature."

But Schlanger, who knows the power hierarchy based in the West, from study as well as long practice, emphasizes that the strings of what is now Jerry Brown's fascist policy imposed on California, are pulled from well above Brown's level.

"Brown's fascist, population-reduction policy is also coherent with the so-called conservatives, in particular Pete Wilson [California governer 1991-99—ed.], and then Arnold Schwarzenegger [governor 2003-07—ed.], both of whom have very green sides to them, especially Schwarzenegger. Social liberal, in the case of Jerry Brown ... in terms of gay rights and things of that sort, but in terms of science policy, it's anti-science, anti-population. And we can't look at this in terms of this period from the Nixon Administration to the present, without seeing the big shadow of George Shultz, from the Hoover Institution at Stanford, as a godfather to most of the California governments over that period of time."

George Shultz's War on FDR

The State of California, despite its importance to the Union going back to its entry just before the Civil War, was built by President Franklin Roosevelt (see following article). The state had only one-tenth of its current population before FDR took office, and the world-famous Central Valley food-production powerhouse was inhabited by only a few tens of thousands of human beings.

This is the condition to which Jerry Brown's water

FIGURE 1
Proposed Locations for 42 Nuclear Desalination Plants

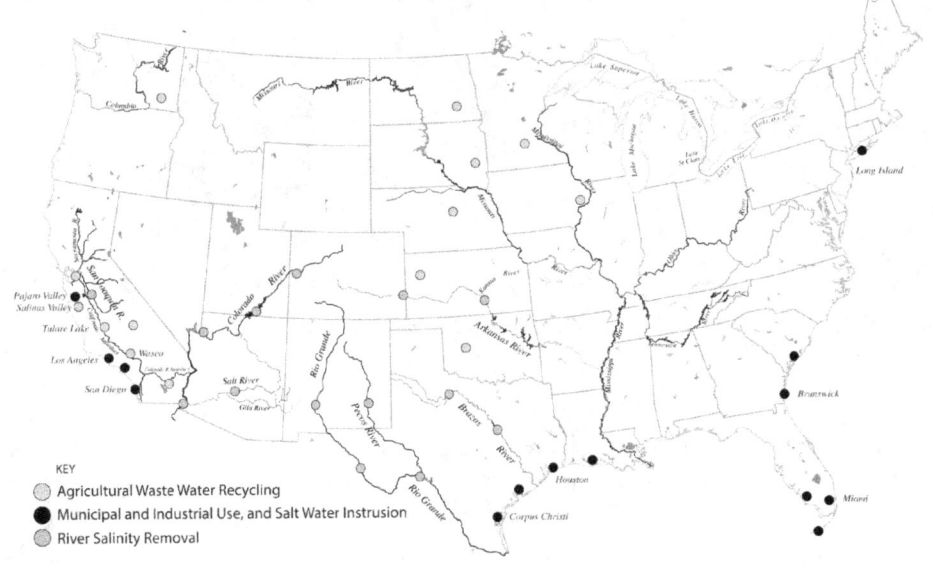

KEY
- Agricultural Waste Water Recycling
- Municipal and Industrial Use, and Salt Water Instrusion
- River Salinity Removal

21st Century Science & Technology, 2013

"Without nuclear, California lacks one of the key immediate means of using the vast Pacific lapping at its 800-mile coast to produce freshwater in quantity for the parched state. It will take five years to create that capacity now, and that will take removing Brown from office immediately; he is as much an anti-nuclear diehard as ever."

cuts could return this incredibly productive state! Brown's 25-35% water cuts are hitting the poorest communities, and those in the most drought-stricken Central Valley areas, the hardest; they will depopulate these areas. Farmers whose acreage is near the towns are *not* exempt from Brown's water-cut mandates, because they get their water from the town water utilities which are ordered to impose the cuts. Millions of acres of farmland will lie fallow in 2015, more even than in 2014. This is being detailed to LaRouchePAC organizers by residents in the Central Valley; and those organizers are testing them: The water *is* there; we have to take it and create it; will you fight for that and dump Brown out of office, or will you try to "conserve until you leave"—or die?

Brown's fascist no-water policy could take the state back to its condition before FDR's great projects brought water from the Colorado River, water from the central California mountains, water, power, and transportation from the Sacramento and San Joaquin rivers.

What FDR did not build of California's superb infrastructure, was built during the governorship of Edmund G. "Pat" Brown, from 1959-67.

"If you look at Jerry Brown's past," Schlanger says, "he broke completely with his father, who was an FDR

What FDR (left) did not build of California's superb infrastructure, was built during the governorship of Edmund G. "Pat" Brown (right), from 1959-67.

Democrat. Jerry Brown, once elected, infamously refused to meet or even to speak to his father, who had gotten him into office. Pat Brown was the governor who basically inaugurated California into the modern era, with his infrastructure projects, water projects, improvement of the educational system, the advancement of industry and industrialized agriculture in the state. [Jerry] Brown turned against all of them with his 'small is beautiful' philosophy, and then also, brought in as special advisor in his first administration, Stewart Brand ... an anti-science, anti-government type who said, 'We need to enter an era of limits.' Brand had previously been one of the Merry Pranksters, known for dropping LSD in the punch at parties."

But George Shultz was the anti-FDR godfather who installed one California governorship after another, from his bases at the Hoover Institution at Stanford University, the University of Chicago, the Council of Foreign Relations, the Rocky Mountain Institution, the Bohemian Grove, etc. Shultz, in the early 1970s, as Nixon's Treasury Under Secretary and then Secretary, forced Nixon's abandonment of Roosevelt's Bretton Woods System, creating the modern "global financial casino" in place of stability and growth. Through Chicago, he worked closely with Milton Friedman to introduce fascist policies into Chile, overthrowing President Salvador Allende, replacing him with dictator Agosto Pinochet.

Shultz's father came from the same Morgan/Harriman banking networks as Prescott Bush, and Shultz has always been influential with George H.W. Bush. Shultz and Dick Cheney notoriously "created" the George W. Bush Administration.

Shultz has been prominent, with ex-Treasury Secre-tary Hank Paulson who heads up the green anti-population Nature Conservancy, in the Green Business Alliance launched by British royal green fascist Prince Charles in 2012. Shultz's Rocky Mountain Institution was a big—perhaps the biggest—force behind pushing the subsidizing and mandating of ethanol as auto fuel.

Nazi Puppets

Harley Schlanger was a close observer, opponent, and one of the experts on the Enron "electricity deregulation" catastrophe of 1999-2001. This scandal put electricity prices and "futures" on privatized speculative markets dominated by Enron, the closest single company to the Bush family—after electric utilities had been forced to break up into production and distribution "parts" which could be bought and sold by the same speculators.

Pete Wilson, from the Hoover Institution, was the Shultz governor (1995-99) who put California under electricity deregulation. Wilson's action was as destructive as it was because California, by the 1990s, was drastically short of electrical power generating capacity. And that was the work of the anti-nuclear, green fascist administration of Shultz governor Jerry Brown—the first time around.

Besides repeated blackouts and the loss of the entire aluminum industry in the Northwest, the deregulation crisis forced poorer people to lose power entirely as prices per kilowatt-hour skyrocketed higher and higher. Schlanger reports, "We estimated at the time that $70 billion was taken from California by the [electricity-trading] corporations, Enron and some of the others; and the state had to come up with some of that money. But the other effect was that poor and elderly people couldn't afford air conditioning in the hot Summer of 2000." When Shultz and Cheney's "W" Bush came in in 2001, Cheney refused all aid, "saying, 'We think this is a matter for the free market.'"

The Enron debacle was manipulated to push Democratic Gov. Gray Davis (1999-2003) out in a recall. Cartoon actor Arnold Schwarzenegger was picked out of Hollywood by Shultz (and Ted Kennedy, uncle to Schwarzenegger's wife) and taken to meetings at Lord Jacob Rothschild's English mansion to be vetted and prepared to replace Davis.

George Shultz's fascist puppets, left to right: Pete Wilson, Arnold Schwarzenegger, Jerry Brown, George W. Bush

At those meetings, Schwarzenegger got the stamp of approval of Rothschild and British Royals, and Warren Buffett. "What they saw in Schwarzenegger was someone who they thought would have the toughness, the lack of human compassion to be willing to kill people with budget cuts," says Schlanger. "He also governed along the same lines as Jerry Brown's first two terms, as a greenie." Schwarzenegger's well-known earlier comments admiring the career of Adolf Hitler were put down as "youthful indiscretion." With Davis tarred with the Enron disgrace that Shultz's Pete Wilson had launched, Schwarzenegger got in, vowing war with labor unions, medical providers, Medicaid patients, and lower-middle-income citizens generally, to make "Cullyfornia" friendly for big business.

"Schwarzenegger," recalls Schlanger, "brought in as his financial advisor Donna Arduin, who had been [Florida governor] Jeb Bush's budget director.... As they said in Florida, 'She cut to the bone, if not into the bone,' cutting programs for the poor and elderly, education, dental and vision plans for children in poor families."

After four years in office, "Terminator" Schwarzenegger was sufficiently hated by Californians that the trick could be pulled yet again: Shultz governor Jerry Brown came back into office as anybody-but Shultz governor Schwarzenegger.

Now Shultz has formed a "Hoover Intitute-Silicon Valley" alliance with hedge fund billionaire Tom Steyer, to implement carbon limits and carbon "trading" in California. The rubric is "Future 500," and it also advises on "water stewardship." Future 500 currently features on its site an interview with World Wildlife Fund Board Member Alexis Brown, who says about California's drought: "The win isn't solving the drought; rather, the goal is to get people to share water resources and work together to make best use of these limited resources for the well-being of humans and nature."

To Jerry Brown's economic advisors—one of whom wanted to call the police on author Michael Steger for disagreeing that the deepening drought is caused by CO_2 emissions—Silicon Valley now *is* California's economy. They view the Central Valley, where 30% of America's vegetables, and much of its other produce, are grown, as "just 2% of GDP."

But water is not "GDP"; it is economy and food and life. Prohibiting "solving the drought," when human science and ingenuity could solve it, is anti-human. Schlanger calls it "a Nazi policy, which starts from the idea of eliminating useless eaters, or reducing population using whatever means are at hand—coming from very high-level Wall Street operatives, who have used California as a testing ground for a long time, for introducing crazy ideas which are designed to brainwash a population into rejecting the orientation of science and technology which characterized the best moments in California."

How Franklin Roosevelt and Pat Brown Built California

by Robert Ingraham

The following article was written for The New Federalist newspaper in 2005 but was never published.

Writing in "Cauchy's Infamous Fraud," (*EIR,* April 1, 2005) Lyndon LaRouche defined what he calls "The Noösphere Principle." LaRouche says that the progress of mankind is defined by "a principle of endless, and accelerating scientific and related progress," and that this is a fundamental and universal truth, to which all nations and governments must cohere. The role of government is not to be a referee, impotently overseeing economic looting by private interests in some free-market system designed during a masturbatory fantasy of an Ayn Rand cultist. Government's role is to ensure that human progress, including the technologically driven development of the physical economy, continues.

As a case study, the state of California demonstrates exactly how magnificent the sovereign power of government, if utilized in the way LaRouche describes, can be. The current decimation of California under the hammer blows of the Bush Administration, and the pro-Hitler then-Governor Arnold Schwarzenegger, only accentuates the need to return to the policies that built California, and the nation, during the 20th Century.

Beginning in 1933, under Franklin Roosevelt, and continuing for more than 30 years, particularly under Gov. Pat Brown (1959-67), the entire physical economy and the biosphere of California were transformed. Rivers were moved, mountains were tunneled, harbors were developed, energy was harnessed, and thousands of bridges, dams, canals, generating stations, parks, schools, and hospitals were built. Much of this was accomplished with breathtaking speed. Out of this process modern California was born.

I. What Franklin Roosevelt Accomplished

The Water Projects

In 1930, California was an undeveloped, underpopulated, and largely unindustrial state, within which immense geographical areas were nothing but semi-desert backwaters. Los Angeles, although a large city, was still smaller than San Francisco, and, with a population of 576,000, was barely larger than Buffalo, N.Y. San Jose, today the center of Silicon Valley, was a city of only 45,000, and the great Central Valley was practically empty, with Bakersfield, a town of only 24,000, and Modesto, a village of a mere 9,000. That all changed, beginning in 1933.

During Roosevelt's first year in office, Secretary of the Interior Harold Ickes announced that the Administration would escalate the Boulder Dam project—the construction of a dam and reservoir on the Colorado River—with the intent to finish it two years early. The Boulder (later renamed Hoover) Dam, together with the Tennessee Valley Authority, and the projects on the Columbia and St. Lawrence rivers, were the great "Four Corners" infrastructure projects of Roosevelt's New Deal.

In early 1934, Ickes allotted $38 million, through the Bureau of Reclamation (BOR), in order to finish the dam ahead of schedule. Construction was completed in less than one year, and the reservoir began to fill on Feb. 1, 1935. Hydroelectric generation began in September 1936. Originally 12 generators produced 3 billion kilowatt hours of electricity annually (1/8 of all U.S. electricity generation in 1940). Five more generators were added in 1961. Contracts with the Metropolitan Water

District of Southern California and the Southern California Edison Company supplied both water and power to southern California.

The Hoover Dam was 726 feet high, and took 750,000 cubic yards of concrete to build (enough to build a six-lane highway from Seattle to New York City). Behind the dam was Lake Mead, the world's largest artificial lake, 115 miles long and 500 feet deep, holding 28.5 million acre-feet of water.

From the dam, two canals were built to bring water into Southern California. Together they revolutionized both agriculture and urban development in the southern part of the state. The first of these was the All-American Canal, an 80-mile artery from the Colorado River into California's Imperial Valley along the Mexican border. Begun in 1934 with a grant of $9 million from FDR's Public Works Administration (PWA), the canal was completed in 1940. In 1942, a second branch—a 130-mile canal—was extended to the north, into the Coachella Valley. The water from these two canals brought 1.5 million acres of land under cultivation and transformed the region into the "Winter Garden of America." Both were built by the Interior Department's Bureau of Reclamation, at a total cost of $24 million, with the money to be repaid by the two local water districts over 40 years at zero interest, a practice common to FDR's water projects.

The second major waterway from the Hoover Dam was the 300-mile-long Colorado River Aqueduct. Financed by a $220 million loan from Jesse Jones' Reconstruction Finance Corporation (RFC), and built by the Metropolitan Water District of Southern California, construction of the aqueduct required crossing desert wastelands and tunneling through mountains, in order to bring water to the City of Los Angeles.

In addition to the water projects, the Los Angeles Bureau of Power and Light received Federal money to build high-tension electric lines from Hoover Dam's generators to supply electricity to the city.

FDR Library

The Boulder (later renamed Hoover) Dam, together with the TVA, and the projects on the Columbia and St. Lawrence rivers, were the great "Four Corners" infrastructure projects of Roosevelt's New Deal. Here, FDR looks over construction of the dam, September 1935.

The final part of the Colorado project was the construction, 155 miles below Hoover Dam, of the Parker Dam. Financed by a loan from the RFC, it too was built by the Metropolitan Water District of Southern California. This dam supplied electricity to both Southern California and Phoenix, Ariz.

The Central Valley Project

Extending from the Tehachapi Mountains north of Los Angeles to the Shasta Mountains north of Redding, California's Central Valley is 500 miles long and 125 miles wide. At 62,500 square miles, it encompasses an area greater than the combined size of Massachusetts and Pennsylvania. In 1932, it had a population of less than 900,000.

Plans to develop the water potential of the valley originated in the 1870s, when Col. Barton Alexander of the U.S. Army Corps of Engineers was deployed to California by President Ulysses S. Grant. In 1919, Col. Robert Bradford Marshall, the Chief Hydrographer of the U.S. Geological Survey, presented a detailed water plan which formed the initial basis of what eventually became the Central Valley Project (CVP).

Marshall's 1919 plan included the following components: 1) a dam on the northern Sacramento river, with two canals to bring water to the delta; 2) a pumping station in the delta to send water into a canal down the Central Valley; 3) a dam on the American River near Folsom, with a canal to the same Delta pumping station; 4) a dam on the San Joaquin River northeast of Fresno, with two canals, one northward and the other southward to Bakersfield; 5) a Contra Costa Canal to deliver water into the East Bay region (east of Oakland).

In 1921, the state legislature funded a $200,000 study by the State Engineer on the feasibility of the Marshall Plan. The Engineer's final recommendations (very close to Marshall's original plan) were officially adopted in 1931. In 1933, the legislature created the Central Valley Project, and in December of that year, California voters approved the sale of $170 million in bonds to build it.

At that point, the project stopped dead in its tracks. In the Depression year of 1933, the state could find no buyers for the bonds. Not one of them was sold, and the project languished for more than two years. In 1935, the Roosevelt Administration stepped in, and announced that the Federal government would assume the responsibility for the construction of Shasta Dam, the most important single component of the project. In 1936, both houses of the California legislature voted to ask the Federal government to take over and build the entire Central Valley Project. In August of 1937, Congress approved the Central Valley Project Act, and authorized PWA grants to get it started. The CVP, and all of its components, became a project of the Federal Bureau of Reclamation.

What Was Built

At the heart of the Project was a plan to develop the two main river systems which feed the Central Valley, the Sacramento and San Joaquin rivers. Major dams, reservoirs, and generating stations were to be built on both rivers. The various tributaries of these rivers would also be developed and integrated into the overall plan. These included the American, Feather, Pitt, York, and Bear rivers (tributaries of the Sacramento River), and the Fresno, Merced, Tuolumne, Stanislaus, and Chowchilla rivers (tributaries of the San Joaquin River).

The key component for the entire project was the Shasta Dam on the Northern Sacramento River. Begun in 1937 with labor from the Federal Works Progress

FIGURE 1

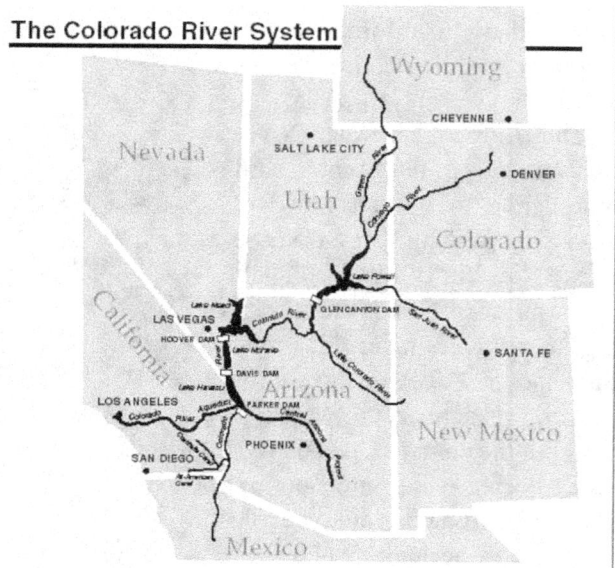

The Colorado River System

Administration (WPA), Shasta Dam was completed in 1944. It was the second-largest concrete dam in the World, after the Grand Coulee. By comparison, the Hoover Dam was taller, at 726 feet, than Shasta's 602, but Hoover was only 1,282 feet wide, compared to Shasta's 3,500 feet. The Shasta Dam delivers 4.5 million acre-feet of freshwater per year, and its turbines produce 1.5 billion kilowatt hours of electricity annually. From Shasta, water flows south on the Sacramento River to the Keswick Dam.

The development of the American River contained two separate projects. The first was the Folsom Dam project. Originally authorized in 1944, construction was delayed by the war. Eventually, the dam was built by the Army Corps of Engineers, from 1951 to 1956, and then turned over to the Bureau of Reclamation. The Folsom unit includes Folsom Dam, Folsom Lake, and a power plant, as well as Nimbus Dam, Lake Natoma, and a power plant. The second part of the American River Project was the Sly Park unit, which includes the Sly Park Dam, Jenkensen Lake, the Camp Creek Diversion Dam and Tunnel, and the Camino Conduit and Tunnel. Today, the entire American River Project delivers 1 million acre-feet of water annually into the CVP system.

Most of the water from the Shasta and Folsom dams flows through the 50-mile-long Delta Cross Channel. In Tracy, half of that water is pumped into the Delta-Mendota Canal, and then flows 117 miles to the south. The Tracy pumps are powered by electricity from the

Shasta, Folsom, and Keswick turbines. Other water from Tracy is pumped into the Contra Costa Canal, built in 1937, which brings water into the San Francisco-East Bay region from the delta.

The second major component of the Central Valley Project was the development of the San Joaquin River system, anchored by the construction of Friant Dam, northeast of Fresno. Built between 1939 and 1944, water from the Friant Dam is diverted into two canals, the Madera Canal (to the north) and the Friant-Kern Canal, which flows 154 miles south to Bakersfield, and irrigates the whole eastern side of the San Joaquin Valley. Both of these canals were completed in 1951.

By 1961, the CVP included 7 dams, 390 miles of canals, 4 power plants, 8 pumping stations, and 760 miles of transmission lines. It delivered over 3 million acre-feet of water annually for irrigation and other uses, and over 3 billion kilowatt hours of electricity.

To accomplish these construction projects required an infinite variety of heavy equipment and machinery, all supplied by American manufacturing plants.

The Project, however, was still not complete. Later phases included: 1961—Trinity Reservoir, which diverts 865,000 acre-feet of Trinity River water south to the Sacramento Valley system; 1965—the 125-mile-long Tehama-Colusa Canal, covering Tehama, Glenn, Colusa, and Yolo counties, northwest of Sacramento; 1968—the San Luis Unit, on the west side of the San Joaquin Valley, near Kettleman City. This includes the New Melones Reservoir on the Stanislaus River, and was intended to tie in with the (still un-built) Auburn Dam system; 1961-62—various Army Corps of Engineers projects: Pine Flats Reservoir (on the Kings River), Isabella Reservoir (on the Kern River), Success Dam (on the Tule River), and Terminus Dam (on the Kaueah River).

By 1975, the CVP included 40 dams and storage reservoirs, more than 25 canals (covering over 2,000 miles), and 28 hydroelectric plants. Three million acres of new land were put into production. The total cost of both phases was $2 billion. Today, California's Central Valley contains more than 20% of all the irrigated land in the United States.

Creative Commons/Robert Campbell

The Shasta Dam was the single-most important component of the Central Valley Project, which got underway in 1937, under the auspices of the Bureau of Reclamation.

II. Transforming the Biosphere

In reading over all the dates, facts, and numbers in the previous section, it is easy to fog out and to miss the magnitude of what was accomplished in California. However, please consider the following: The 80-mile-long All-American Canal, itself only one (relatively small) component of California's man-made water system, delivers more acre-feet of water per year to the Imperial Valley, than the annual flow of the Potomac River past Washington, D.C. Between 1933 and 1945, the State of California was transformed in a way that no other location on Earth has ever been changed by the intervention of man, within such a short time. Don't think "infrastructure projects"; think instead "terraforming."

A myriad of Federal agencies were deployed by the Roosevelt Administration to get the job done. These included:

1. The Interior Department's Bureau of Reclamation: the primary agency which had oversight over almost all the major water and irrigation projects in the western United States, including the Hoover Dam and the Central Valley Project.

2. The Works Progress Administration: Between 1935 and 1943, the WPA employed 8,500,000 people in more than 1,400,000 projects throughout America. Nationally, it built 651,000 miles of roads and highways; constructed or repaired 124,000 bridges and 125,000

public buildings (including hospitals, TB wards, libraries, schools, and post offices). It constructed 853 airport landing fields, and 8,200 parks.

3. The Public Works Administration (PWA): It played a key role in financing the construction of thousands of schools, hospitals, bridges, government office buildings, and other facilities during roughly the same period as the WPA.

4. The Army Corps of Engineers: Among its other functions, the Corps was responsible for flood-control projects. In that capacity, it built hundreds of dams across the country. Since it was not allowed to be involved in irrigation projects, and the Bureau of Reclamation was not supposed to be involved in flood control, the two agencies often functioned in tandem. In the Central Valley Project, the BOR built the major irrigation and hydroelectric dams, but many of the smaller dams were built by the Corps of Engineers.

5. The Rural Electrification Administration: Established May 11, 1935 by Executive Order, and authorized by Congress in 1936, the REA was placed under the Agriculture Department. It made long-term, low-interest loans to state and local governments and farmers' cooperatives. Between 1935 and 1941, millions of farms, rural communities, and businesses, which the private utilities refused to service, were provided with electricity.

6. Many other agencies, including the Civilian Conservation Corps, which aided in forest reclamation. (During the New Deal, over 2 billion trees were planted in the U.S.A.).

In the State of California some, among the many, accomplishments of the men and women of these agencies were:

1. The San Francisco-Oakland Bay Bridge: Construction began in July 1933, and was completed in November 1936. The total cost of the bridge was $78 million. The initial funding came from a $62 million loan from the RFC. The bridge was completed ahead of schedule after securing an additional $16.2 million grant from the Public Works Administration. The Bay Bridge was the most expensive public works project in U.S. history up to that time.

2. The Caldecott Tunnel: Another PWA project, this tunnel is familiar to anyone who has lived in the Bay Area. It goes through the coastal range east of Oakland and connects the interior of Alameda and Contra Costa counties to the Bay Area. It opened on Dec. 5, 1937.

3. The development of Stockton as a deep water

Newscom

Southern California's great Imperial Valley. "Between 1933 and 1945, the State of California was transformed in a way that no other location on Earth has ever been changed by the intervention of man, within such a short duration of time."

port. Stockton Channel, begun in 1930 and completed in 1933 made Stockton, on the San Joaquin River, a deep water port, capable of handling ocean-going cargo vessels. From 1933 to 1940, vast improvements, including dredging, were completed with PWA funds.

4. In 1933, after the Long Beach earthquake, practically the entire city was rebuilt with WPA and PWA funds.

5. The rebuilding of the entire Los Angeles County School System between 1934 and 1938, including the construction of 140 brand new schools and 536 school buildings. Over half the money came from the PWA. High schools included South Pasadena, Emerson, Thomas Jefferson, and Hollywood, as well as Pasadena City College.

6. From 1934 to 1938, more than 221 major new government office buildings were built in California by the PWA, including the Alameda County Courthouse on Lake Merritt in Oakland, central post offices (including in San Francisco and Santa Monica), the Los Angeles Union Station (the last great train station built in the United States), and Long Beach Airport.

7. In 1939, following the flood of 1938, which killed 49 people and buried large sections of the city under water, the entire Los Angeles River System was rebuilt by the Army Corps of Engineers. This involved major relocation and upgrading of the Los Angeles River, Rio Honda, and the San Gabriel River. Consider that in one single year, 1936-37, the following

projects were simultaneously under construction in California:

- The Colorado River Aqueduct
- The All-American Canal
- Shasta Dam
- San Francisco-Bay Bridge
- Oakland-Bay Bridge
- Golden Gate Bridge
- Hundreds of WPA & PWA projects (schools, libraries, hospitals, post offices, etc.)
- Rural electrification

As a result of the in-depth development of California's infrastructure, by the end of Roosevelt's second term, the state had become a national leader in technology and manufacturing. In 1939, Los Angeles County led the nation in agricultural production and in the manufacture of aircraft. It was second in automobile assembly and third in oil refinery. During World War II this development continued, even escalated. From 1941 to 1945, the U.S. government invested $70 billion in capital projects in California, mostly in Los Angeles and San Diego counties. Whole new industries were created. Between 1940 and 1943, the population of California increased by 40%.

In 1945, the five largest dams in the world were the Grand Coulee, Shasta, Fontana, Boulder, and Friant—all built under Franklin Roosevelt. Of these, Shasta and Friant were in California, and Hoover (on the Arizona-Nevada border) serviced the southern part of the state.

III. 'Pat' Brown's Fight To Continue FDR's Work

Shortly after winning the 1958 gubernatorial election, Democrat Edmund G. "Pat" Brown told a gathering of supporters, "I would pray that my works as Governor would reach the most forgotten person in the state of California." More than any single accomplishment of his career, that brief sentiment by Brown reveals the true measure of a remarkable political leader.

In high school, Pat Brown had organized his own fraternity, because the main fraternity excluded Jews (Brown was a Catholic). As San Francisco's District Attorney in the 1940s, he urged the adoption of laws to ban racial discrimination in housing. Later, as Califor-

Gov. "Pat" Brown (1959-67), an FDR Democrat, vowed that he would build the largest infrastructure project ever attempted in a single state in U.S. history. And he delivered.

nia's Attorney General, he issued a ruling that the racially segregated Los Angeles firehouses were unconstitutional, and he also acted against the mistreatment of patients at the state's mental hospitals, and aggressively supported prison reform.

In 1959, during his first year as governor, Brown signed into law the creation of the Fair Employment Practices Commission. A 1956 study had shown that of California's seven major oil companies, only one employed blacks in white-collar jobs; California's four largest brewers employed no blacks at all; there were no black employees, except as waiters and waitresses, in all of the top hotels in Los Angeles; and every major department store had an all-white sales force.

When Martin Luther King visited Los Angeles, Brown personally headed up the invitations committee. At about the same time he publicly donated $100 to the Mississippi Freedom Riders, and when he was criticized in the *Los Angeles Times* for supporting "troublemakers," he stood his ground. On Jan. 7, 1963, in his second inaugural address, Brown said, "A century has passed since Lincoln promised the slaves that they would be 'forever free'.... In conscience we cannot say today that we have redeemed Lincoln's promise." In the months that followed, Brown, together with Assemblyman Byron Rumford (one of only two African-Americans in the state legislature), pushed through the landmark Fair Housing Bill, outlawing racial discrimination in housing. When that law was repealed the next year by passage of Proposition 14 in a state referendum, Brown told the media, "You can draw but one conclusion from the vote on 14, and that is that the white man is just afraid of the Negro. The Negroes have a long way to go before there is any acceptance by the white majority in our state."

As governor, Brown was responsible for a massive expansion of the state's public university and college system. During his first term, he increased aid to public schools, enacted state-funded health care for 9,000 poor, disabled persons, raised disability benefits, raised unemployment benefits, enacted the biggest tax increase in 25 years (primarily on the rich and corporations), and defeated all attempts to impose budget cuts. He enacted major Civil Rights legislation. He increased funding for social programs, for those most defenseless and in need, and supported public housing. He imposed a four-year moratorium on the death penalty.

It was also under Gov. Pat Brown that the state's first commercial nuclear power plant—the Humboldt Bay Nuclear Power Plant—was opened in 1963. An unshakeable commitment to the general welfare shines through as an unbroken thread throughout the entirety of Pat Brown's long political career.

The State Water Project

Passing over the Tehachapi Mountains on Interstate 5, a traveler from Los Angeles descends into California's magnificent Central Valley. For hundreds of miles, almond groves, peach orchards, tomato fields, grape vines, cotton fields, and thousands of acres containing a bounty of crops flank the freeway. Along this route,

FIGURE 2

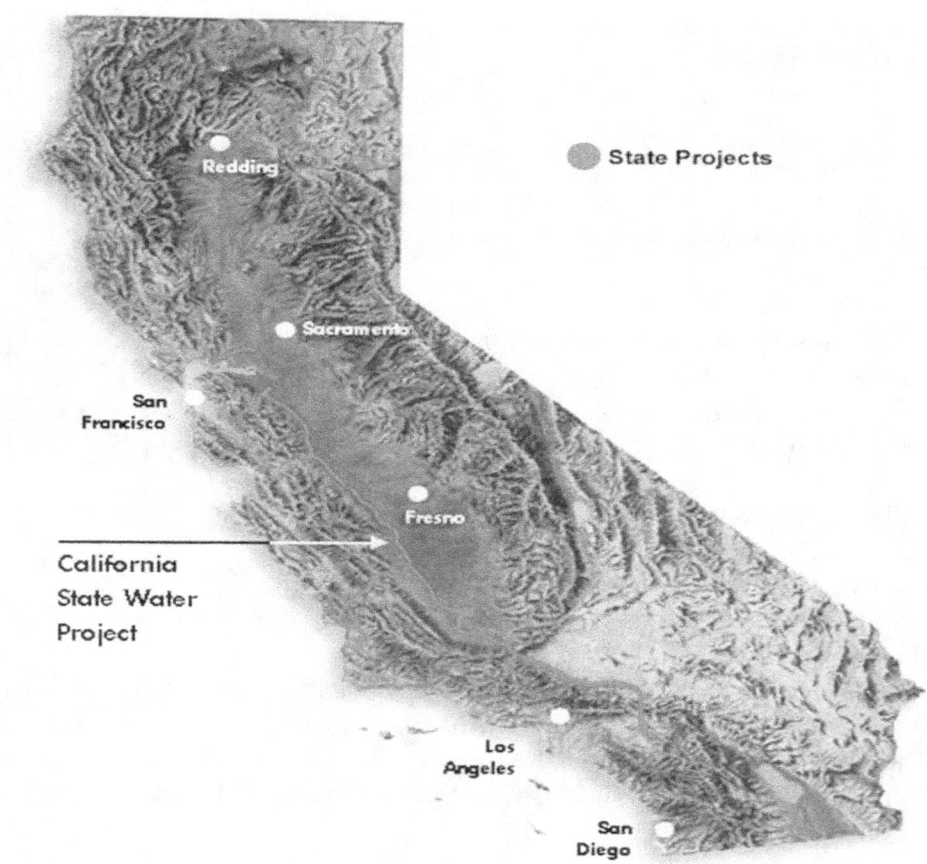

California State Water Project

from Bakersfield north to the California Delta—a distance of more than 250 miles—a man-made river runs alongside the freeway. That river is the Edmund G. Brown Aqueduct, named after California's greatest governor of the 20th Century.

In 1958, Brown campaigned for governor on primarily one issue: *that he would build the largest infrastructure project ever attempted by any individual state in the history of the United States.* Originally known as the Feather River Project, what Brown built is known today as the State Water Project (SWP), a massive complex of 32 reservoirs, 17 pumping stations, 662 miles of canals, the great California Aqueduct, and the Oroville Dam.

Originally proposed in 1951 as a complement and extension of the Central Valley Project, the Feather River Project was blocked by the dead hand of Hiram Johnson, the originator of California's "direct democracy" method of government. Under the Initiative and

Referendum process, foisted on the state in the early 20th Century by populist Gov. Hiram Johnson (1911-17), any major state-funded construction project, including major water projects, required an amendment to the California Constitution. This meant a two-thirds vote of the state legislature and approval by the California voters. As a result, the Feather River proposal was bottled up in the legislature from 1955 through 1958.

In 1958, during a post-election press conference, Governor-elect Brown simply announced that, in his view, a constitutional amendment was not required, and that he would proceed without one. Seven months later, by simple majority vote, the legislature passed the Burns-Porter Act authorizing the state government to borrow $1.75 billion—a staggering amount equal to more than 75% of the entire state budget—and build the project. Brown was still forced to get voter approval, and for almost a year, against intense political opposition, he criss-crossed the state, campaigning for the ballot initiative to approve the plan. On Nov. 8, 1960, the same day that John F. Kennedy was elected President, California voters approved Brown's plan by a vote of 5,842,712 to 5,668,768, a margin of only 174,000 votes.

The centerpiece of the project was the Oroville Dam on the Feather River. When completed in 1967, the Oroville Dam, together with the already existing Shasta and Folsom dams, made possible the creation of the "Delta Pool" as the key to the state's man-made water system. The backbone of the water-delivery system became the new California Aqueduct, which travels south from the Delta through the Central Valley. This was completed in 1968. In northern California, the South Bay Aqueduct was built. This brought water into the Livermore Valley in 1962, and into Santa Clara Valley (today's Silicon Valley) in 1965.

The great California Aqueduct, which now bears Brown's name, was a massive project which, when completed, carried three times the volume of water of the earlier Delta-Mendota Canal, which had been built by the Federal government as part of the Central Valley Project. These two man-made rivers run down the Central Valley and then join at the San Luis Reservoir.

Crossing the Mountains

From the San Luis Reservoir, 2 million acre-feet of water pour south in a single mighty channel, finally ar-riving at the Tehachapi Mountain Range. From there, four gigantic pumps, combined with a series of centrifugal pumps, send the water straight up from the valley floor, 3,000 feet over the mountain peaks. The water then flows through a series of tunnels and channels into three reservoirs—one at Pyramid Dam, a second at Castaic Dam, and a third at the Perris Reservoir. This last required a route that travels over the 3,000-feet Mojave and Antelope Plateaus, crossing and re-crossing the San Andreas Fault, ending at the Cedar Springs Reservoir.

From there, a four-mile tunnel takes the water to Devil Canyon near San Bernadino, goes underground, and emerges at the Perris Reservoir. All of the water that crosses the Tehachapi and arrives in these reservoirs, goes to Los Angeles and other cities in the Southland (the greater Los Angeles area).

The State Water Project was breathtaking in scope. It affected communities in the state from Plumas County in the far north, all the way down to the Mexican border. By 1994, the SWP consisted of 32 reservoirs, 17 pumping stations, and 662 miles of canals. It was Pat Brown who pushed the project through. When faced with op-

An aerial photo of the great California Aqueduct, which now bears Governor Edmund G. Brown's name.

ing in our current era of radical, deregulated, free-market economics, characterized by a fanatical commitment to oligarchical "property rights." That same President Nixon, in 1973, signed into law the Endangered Species Act, making the cult of environmentalism the law of the land. This latter development has had a particularly pernicious effect on California.

In taking up the challenge to continue the work of Franklin Roosevelt and Pat Brown, it will not be sufficient, however, to merely complete already planned projects, nor to limit what must be done to

position, he pointed to the California State Code, which says that "all un-appropriated water belongs to all of the people." When the cost of the project jumped to $2.5 billion, Brown issued an Executive Order to sell the $325 million in revenue bonds that had been authorized in 1933 for the original Central Valley Project, but never sold!

IV. Unfinished Business

To this day, both the Central Valley Project and the State Water Project remain unfinished. In 1965, the Auburn-Folsom South Unit, intended to be the crowning jewel of the CVP, was begun, but construction of the Auburn Dam—which would have been the largest arched concrete dam in the world—was halted in 1971. Major components of the State Water Project, including the Peripheral Canal and Eel River Project, were never built.

The dirigist development of the state's water and other natural resources fell victim to the twin insanities that were unleashed on America in the 1970s. On Aug. 15, 1971, President Richard Nixon abolished Franklin Roosevelt's Bretton Woods monetary system, usher-

water development or other "hard" infrastructure projects. Among the urgent needs of the state are the following:

• Major rebuilding and expansion of energy/electricity generation, with a particular focus on nuclear power (including nuclear-powered water desalination).

• Transportation, both inter-city and regional, including high-speed/maglev rail service connecting the state's major urban areas, as well as local mass transit systems.

• Emergency action to address the state's acute health-care crisis. The recent devastation of the state's public-health facilities, including the multiple closures of trauma centers and emergency rooms, must be reversed.

• The state's public education system must be rebuilt from the ground up, with new schools, and adequate funding for teachers, books, and staff.

Were the political resolve mobilized to undertake these projects—in addition to similar urgent tasks in other parts of the country—this would require a marshalling of all the nation's productive capabilities. The re-tooling and rebuilding of America's machine-tool and manufacturing capabilities must by accomplished in the manner proposed by Lyndon LaRouche.

Dr. Natalia Vitrenko

Facing Terror Under a Kiev Regime 'Both Nazi and Fascist'

Natalia Vitrenko, doctor of economics, is a prominent political figure in Ukraine. She is currently chairman of the Progressive Socialist Party of Ukraine (PSPU) and head of the All-Ukraine Public Women's Organization Dar Zhizni (Gift of Life). She also served as People's Deputy of Ukraine in the second and third convocations of the Supreme Rada (Parliament). She replied in writing on April 20, 2015 to questions sent to her by EIR.

The interview followed official threats to Dr. Vitrenko and her colleagues, and assassinations of leading opponents of the Kiev regime in mid-April (the box reprints her April 16 public statement). Lyndon LaRouche has declared that if any harm comes to Dr. Vitrenko, Assistant Secretary of State Victoria Nuland should be held responsible.

Questions were submitted in several groups, which we summarize here.

Our first set of questions cited Vitrenko's intervention at the European Parliament on Feb. 26, 2014, four days after the violent coup in Kiev, when she warned that leftist parties in Ukraine were being physically attacked, and that "the neo-Nazis, in effect, have established their regime." Today, in April 2015, assassinations and suicides of opposition figures are being reported from Ukraine. We asked how such terror against opponents of the post-coup regime has developed over the intervening months, what is the strength of fascist tendencies in the country, and whether President Petro Poroshenko and the Arseni Yatsenyuk government were doing anything against the fascists and their threats. In a second group of questions, we asked about Poroshenko's image as a

EIRNS/Christopher Lewis

Dr. Natalia Vitrenko gives a press conference in Frankfurt, Germany, on March 1, 2014, exposing the fascist takeover of Ukraine.

relative moderate, whether he were threatened by a coup, and if the United States were doing anything about the activity of fascists in Ukraine.

Thirdly, we asked Vitrenko to review her own political career and the current threats against her life.

Fourthly, we wanted to know if there were any Constitutional protections within Ukraine, or outside pressure to honor UN and European Union conventions, that could help.

Our final set of questions concerned the relationship between Ukraine's current economic collapse and the growth of the fascist movement, as well as the current situation of Russian ethnic and Russian-speaking citizens of Ukraine. We referred to the historical phenomenon of "integral" nationalism in Ukraine, which was developed by the early 20th-Century Mussolini-like figure Dmytro Donstov, but re-

jected by such Ukrainian patriots as the universal genius Vladimir Vernadsky.

Dr. Vitrenko chose to reply with a single essay, which has been translated from Russian by Rachel Douglas.

The Fascist Coup of 2014

When I spoke at the European Parliament on Feb. 26, 2014, I showed that the Euromaidan had been organized in Kiev not for the purpose of bringing European values to Ukraine, but rather to establish a neo-Nazi dictatorship.

Several techniques for coming to power have occurred in world practice:

1. democratic elections;
2. so-called color revolutions;
3. coups d'état using right-wing radical elements, such as Nazis or Islamists;
4. coups d'état by the military.

In 2004, the Orange Revolution made Victor Yushchenko President of Ukraine. It was organized and financed by the West. Yushchenko used his powers to legalize the Ukrainian radical nationalists, make heroes of them, and popularize them to the utmost. Victor Yanukovych, who was elected President in 2010, and the Party of Regions under his leadership, not only failed to act against the neo-Nazi and neo-fascist parties and movements in Ukraine, but even abetted their political popularization and the entry of the neo-Nazi Svoboda Party, first into local councils in western Ukraine, and then, in the Fall of 2012, into the national Parliament.

During Yanukovych's years in office, night-time torch marches, demolition of [Soviet-era] monuments, insults to veterans of the Great Patriotic War,[1] and media promotion of collaborationists from the Organization of Ukrainian Nationalists and Ukrainian Insurgent Army (OUN-UPA) such as [Stepan] Bandera, [Roman] Shukhevych, [Yevhen] Konovalets, and others, became standard features of Ukrainian political life. Government agencies did nothing to hinder the dissemination and popularization of the misan-

Svoboda Party leader Oleh Tyanhybok, known for his 2004 speech denouncing the "Moscow-Jewish mafia that rules Ukraine."

thropic ideology of Ukrainian "integral" nationalism (fascism), formulated by [Mykola] Mikhnovsky, [Dmytro] Dontsov, and [Mykola] Stsiborsky.[2] The heart of this set of beliefs is the notion that a nation is a species in nature, where the strongest will survive. The Ukrainian nation is forged only through struggle. The main enemy is Moscow (Russia). Their slogans are "Ukraine for Ukrainians," "Ukraine above all," "Glory to the nation—death to the enemies!" and "Our power will be terrible to the enemies of Ukraine."

These slogans were further developed during the Euromaidan: *"Moskaliv na nozhi, komunyaku na hillyaku,"* meaning "Knife the Muscovites, hang the Communists."

The Progressive Socialist Party, as well as the women's organization Dar Zhizni, both of which I head, campaigned actively against neo-Nazism and neo-fascism in Ukraine. We led street protests throughout Ukraine, organized conferences at the regional, national, and international level, and I waged a gruel-

---

1. The Great Patriotic War signifies the Eastern Front in Europe during World War II, 1941-45.

2. "British Imperial Project in Ukraine: Violent Coup, Fascist Axioms, Neo-Nazis," *EIR*, May 16, 2014, pp. 23-27.

ing, three-year court fight against the neo-Nazi decree #75/2010,[3] issued by President Yushchenko. We published books and newspapers, posted material online, and warned the world community about the threat ensuing from the political rehabilitation of Nazism and fascism in Ukraine.

But Yanukovych and the Party of Regions had plans to win the 2015 Presidential election by making sure that his runoff opponent would be Svoboda Party leader Oleh Tyahnybok. Therefore they were very tough in putting a stop to our campaign.

Literally from the first day of the Euromaidan, Dec. 1, 2013, its ideological nature was absolutely clear from the numbers **88** and **14**,[4] the red-black Nazi flags[5] and slogans, the swastika, Celtic cross, and Wolfsangel symbols, and the portraits of collaborationists who had been agents of Hitler's Abwehr (Konovalets, Bandera, Shukhevych). The main slogan of the Euromaidan was the Banderite cry "Glory to Ukraine—to the heroes glory!", which had been adopted at the Second Conference of the OUN in April 1941 as the equivalent of Hitler's *"Heil Hitler!—Sieg heil!"*

That day, Dec. 1, 2013, was also when cobblestones, clubs, Molotov cocktails, chains, and burning tires appeared at the "peaceful" Euromaidan. As of Feb. 18, 2014, there were firearms, as well.

Leaders from the United States and the EU countries visited Kiev repeatedly and could see all this with their own eyes.[6] They were also receiving information from social and political activists inside Ukraine. But what suited the United States was a seizure of power in Ukraine according to Scenario 3, listed above. They had prepared and financed this for a long time, and ultimately organized it.

Peaceful protesters against the Maidan coup were burned alive by fascists in the Odessa Trade Unions Building on May 2, 2014, as commemorated in this poster.

Today's Political Terror

After the power of the Euromaidan was legitimized, then political terror, the trampling of democratic rights and freedoms, zombification of the population through the media, political "cleansing" operations (called "lustration"), and the imprisonment or physical annihilation of dissenters, all became the ideology and practice of the new regime.

Ukraine has been drenched in blood by civil war in the Southeast. The Minsk Accords of Feb. 2, 2015, and UN Security Council resolution [#2202] of Feb. 17, 2015 [endorsing those Accords], only slightly calmed the conflict, but did not resolve the fundamental problems from which it arose.

The whole world had been shocked by the events of May 2, 2014 in Odessa, when the participants in a peaceful protest were massacred, burned alive in the Trade Unions Building. On May 9, 2014, a holiday demonstration[7] in Mariupol was fired upon. Who was guilty? Who was punished? Those questions remain unanswered. The Ukrainian ultras were organized into

---

3. Ukrainian Presidential Decree 75/2010, dated January 28, 2010, was titled "On the celebration of participants in the struggle for Ukraine's Independence in the 20th Century." It glorified the OUN-UPA.

4. The figure "88" denotes "Heil Hitler," since "h" is the eighth letter of the alphabet, while "14" refers to a white supremacist slogan, 14 words in length.

5. The Banderite OUN flag is red over black.

6. Natalia Vitrenko, "Ukrainian Patriots Expose EU Support for Neo-Nazi Coup," *EIR*, March 7, 2014.

7. May 9 is the anniversary of Victory over fascism, celebrated the day after VE Day in western Europe.

"volunteer" battalions, armed, and dispatched to the Donbass.[8] The reports on their atrocities and pillaging are stunning. They barely answer to the central authorities. And they are financed by the "oligarchy"—wealthy businessmen.

The reign of terror under the Ukrainian regime is now typified by the recent series of "suicides," followed by outright murders of opposition politicians and journalists: V. Semenyuk-Samsonenko, M. Chechetov, S. Melnyk, A. Peklushenko, S. Valter, O. Kalashnikov, O. Buzyna, and others. Ukrainian Labor Party leader A. Bondarchuk, a People's Deputy of Ukraine in the third and fourth convocations of the Supreme Rada, has been arrested. Slander and persecution by law enforcement agencies continue against the leaders of the Progressive Socialist Party of Ukraine (myself, N. Vitrenko) and the Communist Party of Ukraine (P. Symonenko). Via the Mirotvorets ("Peacekeeper") website, Ukrainian law enforcement people, in gross violation of the presumption of innocence, create an image of tens of thousands of Ukrainian citizens as "enemies of the people," thus inciting the neo-Nazis to physically eliminate those whose names are listed there, as well as members of their families.

My evaluation of the current Ukrainian regime is that it is both Nazi and fascist. It qualifies as "Nazi," because those in power are building a monoethnic state, under slogans like "Ukraine above all," "Glory to the nation—to the heroes glory"; and "fascist," because of the system of governance: the absence of democracy and the harshest possible suppression of dissent.

The outward "moderation" of President Poroshenko does not reflect who he is at heart; he is not truly distinct from the right-wing radicals. It's merely that as President, he does certain work that the radicals could not accomplish in the street: Through his decrees and the bills he has introduced into Parliament, he is continuing to make heroes of those who collaborated with Hitler. He automatically gives heroic status to, and popularizes, the brutal methods of annihilating civilians which the OUN Nazis used, both during the German occupation and afterwards, continuing to terrorize Ukraine until 1956.

_____
8. The Donbass, short for the Donetsk Coal Basin, spans two regions of Ukraine—Donetsk and Lugansk.

Unlike a Nazi with a Molotov cocktail in his hand, the President is supposed to be the guarantor of Constitutional rights. He, and the law enforcement agencies subordinate to him, receive budget allocations for the purpose of defending the rights and freedoms of all the citizens of Ukraine, but in practice it is all used to crank up repression against those they don't like.

Neither the U.S. State Department, nor officials from Western European countries, nor the OSCE, nor the Council of Europe, nor the European Parliament are doing anything whatsoever to counter the neo-Nazi processes in Ukraine. Yet international law (the UN Charter, the Universal Declaration on Human Rights, the International Pact on Civil and Political Rights, the European Convention on the Defense of Human Rights and Basic Freedoms, the Convention on the Prevention and Punishment of the Crime of Genocide, the Durban Declaration, etc.) obligate the world community to intervene in Ukraine's political process and carry out de-Nazification.

The countries of the West, however, are caught between their obligations under international law, and the political demands of the United States.

An Economist in Politics

My political career began in 1994, when I won election to Parliament from the Konotop Electoral District, Sumy Region. Holding a doctoral degree in economics and, from 1996 on, as the leader of a party, the Progressive Socialist Party of Ukraine, I strongly opposed the domestic and foreign policies imposed on Ukraine by the International Monetary Fund. But I not only exposed the negative side of the "IMF reforms"; I also proposed a constructive alternative: a coherent economic program, which I prepared jointly with a group of economists and presented in Parliament in October 1995. I developed and introduced into the Supreme Rada of Ukraine a set of laws for the implementation of this program. In 1998, my party surpassed the 4% level, allowing us to enter Parliament and form our own caucus. In 1999, I became the first woman in the history of Ukraine to run for the Presidency. All the public opinion polls showed that I had a chance of winning in a second round, but the assassination attempt against me on Oct. 2, 1999, and the ensuing media campaign to discredit me, allowed [Leonid] Kuchma to remain in power, while I re-

U.S. Assistant Secretary of State Victoria Nuland and U.S. Ambassador to Ukraine Geoffrey Pyatt with Ukrainian President-elect Petro Poroshenko, in Warsaw, June 4, 2014.

ceived only 11% of the vote.

I n 2004, I ran for President of Ukraine a second time, but the application of color revolution techniques prevented democratic elections.

Besides leading my political party, I have been elected to the leadership of several public organizations. One of them is the All-Ukraine Public Women's Organization Dar Zhizni, founded in 2000. This organization provided humanitarian aid to orphans and engaged in human rights work to defend women against discrimination and problems of daily life.

In April 2014, we decided to direct the capabilities of our women's organization to stepped-up human rights activity. Funds were granted to us by the Russian Fund for the Defense of the Rights of Compatriots Abroad, under a contract we concluded with them, for the purpose of setting up regional human rights defense centers.

This then became the pretext for the Ukrainian Security Service (SBU) to initiate a criminal case against our organization, slander me and our activists, and ascribe to us crimes related to "financing separatists and terrorists." The absurdity of this fraud lies not only in the misrepresentation of our goals, but also in the fact that the organization's accounts were frozen, so that

we were unable to receive a single kopeck from anybody. The SBU, and the media under its control, have distorted everything, despite the fact that I provided our contract and all the required documents, and twice gave detailed testimony during interrogations at the SBU.

At the June 3, 2014 court session regarding the freezing of our account, the SBU and the prosecutor's office were able to counter my facts and arguments only with conjectures, guesses, and fantasies. Nonetheless, in violation of the principle of the presumption of innocence, which is enshrined in Article 62 of the Constitution of Ukraine, other Ukrainian laws, and Ukraine's international obligations, I am being portrayed as an accomplice of terrorists and separatists. This serves to incite right-wing radicals to eliminate me physically.

Therefore I was compelled, on April 14, 2015, to appeal to Ukraine's Prosecutor General V.N. Shokin, demanding that he defend my rights and freedoms: above all, the right to life and the inviolability of my person. There has not yet been any reply.

As for the legality of the activity of our women's organization, it is guaranteed under Article 36 of the Constitution of Ukraine, as well as the Ukrainian Law on Public Organizations. There have been no claims of illegal activity against our organization. There is only the SBU falsification, disseminated for the purpose of persecuting me personally, as well as the activists of our organization.

I am truly grateful to the Schiller Institute and the activists of the LaRouche movement for their support. For two decades now, we have been fighting together for a progressive transformation of humanity, and for peace. This is extremely important for me, and for the Ukrainian public. Those wielding authority in Ukraine now understand, that they will not be able to do away with me quietly.

Ethnic Hatred in an Economic Crisis

The socioeconomic crisis in Ukraine is deepening. The IMF loan, with draconian social-sector conditionalities, only compounds the problems.[9] Citizens' exasperation and outrage is on the rise. But, what will it lead to? On the one hand, the neo-Nazi movements are the bulwark of the current regime, and they are politically or physically eliminating dissent; but, on the other hand, the tens of thousands of right-wing radical militants, who are armed and have the experience of fighting in the Donbass, represent the real threat of a coup along the lines of Scenario 4, above. There is resistance to the fascist tendencies, but the forces are unequal. The repressive machine of the state is more effective in achieving its goals.

My view of the situation of the Russian-speaking and culturally Russian population in Ukraine, is that it is being subjected to ethnocide. For the purpose of implementing Dontsov's ideology of expelling or annihilating the Russian ethnic group, as being alien to these Nazis, the Ukrainian Parliament has declared Russia to be an aggressor nation. While Ukrainian passports do not indicate people's ethnic origin, the census taken 14 years ago showed that there were 8 million ethnic Russians, out of a total population of 48 million at that time, living in Ukraine. Russian speakers, however, made up 58% of the population. The jamming of Russian TV channels, banning of Russian TV programs, cancellation of tours by Russian artists, expunging of Russian language and literature courses from school programs, the Parliament's adoption on April 9, 2015 of laws on "decommunization" (declaring the Soviet regime of 1917-91 to have been criminal in both the USSR and the Ukrainian SSR) and the transformation of the OUN-UPA collaborationists into heroes, all creates a legal basis for a monstrous intensification of ethnocide, since Russia today is the legal successor of the Soviet Union.

I thank you for the opportunity to express my opinion about the situation in Ukraine. Please understand, that there are no simple answers to complex questions. I hope that my replies will help in finding a peaceful resolution of not only Ukraine's problems, but those of all mankind, and to prevent a Third World War.

---

9. Susan Welsh, "IMF Applies 'Greek' Austerity Formula to War-Ravaged Ukraine," *EIR*, March 20, 2015; Natalia Vitrenko, "Report from Ukraine: 'Let us end this nightmare, and turn to building things,'" presentation to Citizens Electoral Council of Australia conference, March 29, 2015.

Ensure Right to Life Or Resign, Poroshenko

Dr. Natalia Vitrenko and Vladimir Marchenko, former members of Parliament and leaders of the Progressive Socialist Party of Ukraine, issued the following statement, addressed to Ukrainian President Petro Poroshenko, on April 16, 2015. The subheads have been added.

The European democracy and European values, promised by the Euromaidan, have in reality been forgotten and trampled upon.

The true essence of those currently in power in Ukraine is Nazism, the physical elimination of dissidents, political repressions, terror in the information sphere, the destruction of the national economy, and social genocide.

We are politicians with enough experience, including as Parliamentarians of Ukraine, to make an evaluation of the current regime. We do this with regret, but the facts compel us to defend justice.

Therefore we appeal to you: Stop supporting neo-Nazism in both policies and ideology, stop making heroes of Hitler's accomplices from the Organization of Ukrainian Nationalists and Ukrainian Insurgent Army (OUN-UPA), both as a political movement and for how they practiced the struggle for "Ukraine's independence."

In the mass media, including on your Channel 5, for more than a year, any dissident views whatsoever have been classified as abetting separatists, infringing on the territorial integrity of Ukraine, and undermining the national security. Political and public figures, scientists and teachers, journalists and writers, and even ordinary citizens of Ukraine, who have advocated, and continue to advocate, preserving the integrity of the country, but envision its protection based on different domestic and foreign policy principles than you, the parliamentary majority, and the government formed thereby do, are immediately branded as enemies of the people, Ukrainophobes, and agents of Putin. Lists of "accomplices of separatists and terrorists" are drawn up and disseminated through the Internet.

Natalia Vitrenko at a rally of her party, the Progressive Socialist Party of Ukraine.

Ukraine Security Service Acts Like SS

The Ukraine Security Service (SBU) and the Ministry of Internal Affairs (MVD) disseminate falsehoods about people who don't suit them, initiate criminal cases against them, put them in prison, and drive them to suicide. Among these, without question, are V. Semenyuk-Samsonenko, M. Chechetov, S. Melnik, A. Peklushenko, A. Bondarchuk, S. Dolgov, A. Mayevsky, D. Denisov, and others. Those in power have directed their repressive discreditation and persecution machine also against N. Vitrenko and P. Symonenko.

For two days in a row, Ukraine has been shaken by the murders of political opponents of the authorities: People's Deputy of Ukraine Oleg Kalashnikov, and the writer and journalist Oles Buzyna. These murders were brutal, provocatory, and, unquestionably, politically motivated.

We believe that the horrors being experienced by the people of Ukraine are linked with the activity of neo-Nazi parties and movements, and the support of their actions by those in power (both in the media, and in law enforcement agencies).

The Laws of Ukraine "On the perpetual commemoration of victory over Nazism during the Second World War, 1939-1945," "On the condemnation of communist and national-socialist (Nazi) totalitarian regimes in Ukraine and the prohibition of propaganda of their symbols," and "On the legal status and honoring of the memory of fighters for Ukraine's independence during the 20th century," adopted April 9, 2015, recognized the regime of the USSR and Ukrainian SSR as criminal, while simultaneously glorifying Hitler's accomplices from the OUN-UPA as participants in the Ukrainian liberation movement, thereby glorifying their forms and methods of fighting their political opponents. Those forms and methods of struggle, and the cases of the millions of innocent civilians—women, children, and old men—who were their victims, were examined at the Nuremberg International Military Tribunals. The whole world shuddered at the truth revealed there. Atrocities committed by members of the OUN-UPA were also exposed during thousands of trials in Ukraine after the end of the Great Patriotic War. These crimes were judged to be so monstrous, that even upon review of the cases after 1991, they were deemed inappropriate for exoneration (rehabilitation) proceedings.

You Must Abide by the Constitution

We have already sent you our open letters, demanding that you not sign the aforementioned laws, since by doing so, you would split Ukraine and trigger a mechanism for the physical annihilation of millions of Ukrainians at the hands of neo-Nazi gangs, which are armed to the teeth. Like their predecessors, they will cover for all such horror, in the name of the struggle for an independent Ukraine. And they will consider the murder of the writer and journalist Oles Buzyna to have been a "great deed," just like the October 24, 1949 murder of the outstanding antifascist writer Yaroslav Halan in Lviv.

Petro Alexeyevich, open up the Constitution of Ukraine and the European Convention on Human Rights and Fundamental Freedoms, and read about your obligations to the citizens of Ukraine, the most important of which is the obligation to guarantee the right to life, safety, and inviolability of every person in Ukraine. The SBU and MVD agencies, which are subordinate to you, are obligated to ensure these guarantees, rather than conducting political repressions.

We demand that you, personally, fulfill your constitutional obligations, or leave the political scene!

The Foundation Stone Has Been Laid For a New World Economic Order

Hamilton's America Revived in New York

by Dennis Speed

> ...for the trumpet shall sound, and the dead shall be raised incorruptible, and we shall be changed.

April 20—The 15 nations represented at *Executive Intelligence Review*'s New York City April 16 seminar, held to officially release the *EIR* Special Report, *The New Silk Road Becomes the World Land-Bridge*, heard two presentations that were completely outside of, not only the stated and implied policies of the Obama/Bush "unitary executive" administrations. The ideas of the "double-barrelled" presentations—the keynote by Helga Zepp-LaRouche, and the ground-breaking presentation by LaRouche "Basement Science Team" member Ben Deniston—each of which presented ideas unique in the participants' experience of "policy briefings"—were also "outside of" most of those nations' own then-present evaluations of international policy.

That is, unfortunately for the moment, as it should be. "The content of policy," *EIR* founder Lyndon LaRouche once wrote, "is the method by which it is made." The method presented at the seminar, and the resultant policy conclusions summarized in that report, resurrect the scientific method of discovery of Johannes Kepler, and that of the American System economist, founding father, and co-author of the U.S. Constitution, Alexander Hamilton. Economic policy today demands mastery of both Kepler and Hamilton, as the prerequisite to knowing how to lead the world away from an otherwise sure path to thermonuclear extinction.

Toward the conclusion of her presentation, a *tour d'horizon* of the nearly unknown "New World" of economic development treaties and actions by the BRICS nations (Brazil, Russia, India, China, and South Africa), Zepp-LaRouche warned: "I believe that we have come to a point in human history, where either we bring the political and economic order into cohesion with the real laws of the universe, of the physical universe, or we are threatened to render ourselves extinct in a nuclear annihilation. *However, I think that in all great traditions, you have this idea that the laws of the universe must be a guidance for our political order on the planet.*"

Deniston's refutation of the population-reducing, fascist content of California Governor Jerry Brown's "water conservation policy"—that is, Brown's explicitly stated belief that the "natural population carrying capacity" of California is somewhere around 300,000 people, instead of the nearly 39 million there ("Jerry Brownshirt's" own bizarre advocacy of the interests of the 1% over the 99%)—specifically introduced the seminar audience to the "solar hypothesis" of scientist Johannes Kepler in order to prove that *there could be no water shortage* in California, or the United States, or anywhere else in the world, for that matter.

Willful, deliberate "climate change" by mankind, utilizing ionization technologies, nuclear desalination, and other methods, must and should occur, based on first understanding the solar and extra-solar processes that actually co-generate both the Earth's atmosphere and water production. Studying the higher, galactic-scale processes that determine the relationship between the solar/extra-solar ("cosmic radiation") origins of the Earth's atmosphere, and the presence of water on the more than ten other planetary bodies that are known or thought to have it, is the path to *prevent* human extinction.

World Water, Not World War

From the inception of the American Republic, the creation and utilization not merely of water, but of water power, including the electrodynamics of water power, had shaped, if not determined, the political policies of Benjamin Franklin, George Washington, and Alexander Hamilton and their anti-Articles of Confederation faction.

Franklin's electricity experiments, Washington's Potomac Company, and Washington/Hamilton's joint project to develop the Paterson, N.J. waterfalls through their Society for Useful Manufactures machine complex—not to mention the Erie Canal, the American "Apollo Project" of the 1780s through 1820s—were the expressions of a science of physical economy that sought to deploy the wealth of the nation as a single, unified national weapon, on behalf of the General Welfare of each and all citizens of the republic.

Hamilton's National Bank, and the U.S. Treasury's issuance of public credit for internal improvements, were the engines intended to foster, increase, and multiply the creative powers of each citizen to thus be, in the words of a contemporary,"more powerful than any monarch, yet with no subjects, save his own nature."

But water, Zepp-LaRouche reminded the New York seminar, is not "an American problem." The drought areas of Africa, Asia, etc., provide the perfect means for a new global economic platform of development, where the interiors of continents are developed for the first time in history, greening deserts around the world. The very idea of moving water from the atmosphere, that primarily falls over the oceans, onto land, and of harnessing the secrets of science to temper the climate system of the planet, is an expression of the idea of universal harmony that Kepler and the great Nicholas of Cusa had advocated.

By thinking of the strategic defense of the Earth, and the greatest capabilities of each nation being recruited to that universal self-interest, mankind were made capable of rising out of its adolescence into a true age of history, rather than remaining in slavery to nature or its own lower inclinations. "War against deserts, yes, but not against people."

The "secret," hiding-in-plain-sight, true history and outlook of the United States Constitution, which shows the BRICS process to be identical with our nation's true interests, is incommensurate with the, not merely moronic, but "Neronic" policy of the present Obama Administration, and its earlier incarnation as the Cheney-Bush Administrations of 2001-09—the "Bum and Bummer" twin-worst Presidencies in American history.

The BRICS Revive Physical-Economy

Zepp-LaRouche had implicitly discussed this difference, and also revealed a surprising "hidden truth" about China's "New Silk Road" policy, in Beijing in February of last year, in a half-hour interview with CCTV on the program "Dialogue," hosted by anchor Yang Rui.

> **Yang:** What's the relevance between Abraham Lincoln and the New Silk Road?
>
> **Zepp-LaRouche:** Well, because it is a system of physical-economy. Nowadays, we are thinking very much in monetarist terms. People think about profit, and that has led the world to its present terrible crisis of a threatened collapse of the financial system. And we have to go back to the idea of physical-economy, which is associated with the industrial revolution of America, which was the result of the policies of Lincoln, who also created a land-bridge across America.

The excitement generated by the seminar presentations was noticeable in the discussion, and in the coverage of the event afterwards. China's Xinhua Press News Agency put out a wire which was reproduced in other media in India and other nations. It read, in part:

> "The BRICS nations ... have united to pursue a policy of economic development not just for their individual countries, but for the benefit of the people of all nations," said the Schiller Institute, a think tank with headquarters both in Germany and U.S., in a report released here at a seminar.
>
> Contrary to the Trans-Pacific Partnership advocated by the Obama administration, which excludes Russia and China, the BRICS-related initiatives, including the Chinese proposed Free Trade Area of Asia and the Pacific are inclusive, the think tank said. At the seminar, Helga Zepp-LaRouche, the think tank's founder, spoke highly of the BRICS, saying the emerging-market bloc "initiated a completely new economic system" which is win-win in nature. In blazing a trail to build the new world economic order, the nations of the BRICS are working toward real

economic development, complete with new credit institutions and major high-technology projects to lift the well-being of all participating countries, the founder said.

Alexander Hamilton's America—not that of the Confederacy, and that distinctive brand of Southern-fried fascism that Wall Street's Prescott Bush and the Bush family, along with Barack Obama, have represented in an unbroken line for 100 years—is once again alive, and aroused in the citizenry. Whether it will prevail, for the world is now the question before our age.

Helga Zepp-LaRouche

Here is Helga Zepp-LaRouche's keynote address (delivered electronically) to a seminar for diplomats and journalists sponsored by Executive Intelligence Review, in New York City, April 16, 2015.

Hello. I greet you.

Let me first express that I really would have liked much, much better to talk to you in person, and unfortunately, a little accident prevented me from coming, but I hope we can talk about these issues in this electronic way.

There is something very, very fantastic happening in the world right now, and those of you in America, who are dependent only on the mainstream media, may have absolutely no inkling of it, because the mainstream media are not reporting that a completely new economic system is emerging. It is emerging with extremely rapid speed. And more than half of humanity is already participating in it.

Now, the system was first initiated by the leaders of the BRICS nations, at the Fortaleza summit in Brazil last July. And they proceeded very quickly to establish the New Silk Road and the Maritime Silk Road, and a whole system of relations with South America, with ASEAN countries, with African countries (**Figure 1**), and in the recent period, even with European countries. And this new model basically establishes a completely new system of relations; it's what Chinese President Xi Jinping often calls a "win-win" policy, or even a "win-win-win" policy, depending how many parties are participating in these projects. And it is based on the idea that, through the development of basic infrastructure,

BüSo

Helga Zepp-LaRouche gave the keynote address to the EIR seminar in New York City, April 16. "I believe that we have come to a point in human history, where either we bring the political and economic order in cohesion with the real laws of the universe, of the physical universe, or we are threatened with extinction in a nuclear annihilation," she said.

of scientific and technological cooperation, and an increase in connectivity among these nations, that this will lead to the mutual benefit of all participating countries.

Now, the annual summit of the Boao Forum [March 26-29] on the island of Hainan—the Boao Forum is the Asian equivalent of what normally takes place in Davos in Switzerland, except the difference is that in Davos, you have a lot of bankers and a lot of monetarists coming together, while this Boao Forum brought together many, many leaders, especially of Asia, who were all interested in real economic development, in infrastructure, and cooperation. And at this forum, President Xi Jinping announced what they are now calling the "One Belt, One Road," which is simply another name for the New Silk Road, or, as we called it in the past, the Eurasian Land-Bridge, and announced a global perspective for development.

This includes huge infrastructure programs: corridors, high-speed railways, waterways, and ports. And this report was declared to be official policy by the National Development and Reform Commission, as well as the Foreign Ministry and the Commerce Ministry of China.

As you can see here (Figure 1), this is a vast, vast network of corridors connecting China, Central Asia, Russia—all the way to Europe. Then, another set of corridors from Central Asia, to West Asia, into the Gulf, and the Mediterranean. Then the 21st-Century Mari-

FIGURE 1

time Silk Road involves sea and land corridors from China, to Southeast Asia, to South Asia, to the Indian Ocean, and to the Pacific. Then other corridors go overland from China to Mongolia, to Russia; another one to Bangladesh, China, India, and Myanmar.

So, what goes along with that is a whole new system, a new world system, of banks and financial credit institutions, to finance these and other projects.

The World (Except the U.S.) Joins the AIIB

People were quite astounded about the sea change which recently took place when the AIIB [Asian Infrastructure Investment Bank] went into the final negotiations about who would be among the founding members, negotiations which concluded a couple of days ago. And lo and behold, the AIIB had 57 founding members.

Now the U.S. government, misjudging the situation dramatically, put utmost pressure on its allies, and also developing countries, under those circumstances, not to be part of the AIIB. And despite this heavy pressure from the U.S., the first country in Europe to join was, of all places, Great Britain, the firm ally of the United States. And when Great Britain joined, you had an avalanche of countries going in the same direction—wanting to become founding members of the AIIB: Germany, France, Italy, Luxembourg, Switzerland, Austria, all the Scandinavian countries—and, Australia, South Korea, New Zealand, and many other Asian countries.

China was very emphatic to point out that, despite the fact that the AIIB obviously has been created as a supplement to the IMF and the World Bank, China does *not* want to turn the AIIB into a geopolitical confrontation with the United States, and they have reiterated, both from the government, and also in leading Chinese publications, many times, the offer that the United States and European countries should join the AIIB, the New Development Bank, and also the projects of the New Silk Road and the Maritime Silk Road. Because China is developing a new model of international relationships, which is all-inclusive, which overcomes and supersedes the concept of geopolitics, which, after all, was the basis for two World Wars in the 20th Century.

The New Development Bank, which is a similar bank, created by the BRICS last year, will be functioning in July, at the next BRICS summit, which will take place in Ufa in Russia. So, at that point, you will have two operational large infrastructure banks. But then you also have the New Silk Road development fund, which has $40 billion; the AIIB and the New Development Bank have initial capital of $100 billion each—but that is just the beginning, starting capital. The New Maritime Silk Road Fund has $20 billion. But then also, the countries of the South Asian region, the SAARC countries, are planning to build their own development bank. The Shanghai Cooperation Organization is building a new bank.

And then, these countries have jointly decided to create something which is called the Contingency Reserve Arrangement [CRA]. Now this is a pool of currency reserves, of $100 billion initially, which was obviously a response to the speculation, conducted during the Asia crisis of 1997, where the currencies of Asian countries were speculated against, by speculators such as George Soros, for example; and in one week, they were driven down by 80%. And it was also a result of the 2008 near-meltdown of the financial system in the Lehman Brothers crisis.

What these countries of the BRICS and related organizations are now doing, is, they have created the CRA, to protect participating countries against speculative attacks, even new financial crises that are to come—and they are shortly to come. The CRA was also the reaction to the fact that the U.S. Congress absolutely refused to change the rules of the IMF and the World Bank, after the 2008 crisis.

These parallel financial organizations were charac-

The five Presidents of the BRICS nations, meeting in Brisbane, Australia, November 2014—Putin, Russia; Modi, India; Rousseff, Brazil; Xi, China; Zuma, South Africa— established a new system of relations, what President Xi calls a "win-win" policy.

terized by Mrs. Denise Leung, from the finance center of the World Resources Institute, this morning on the German government radio, Deutsche Welle. This woman said: Development is absolutely not possible without the AIIB and the New Development Bank, because in Asia alone, there is a need for infrastructure investment, up to the year 2020, of $8.2 trillion.

Now, the entire investment of the World Bank, in 2014, was only $24.2 billion, and of the Asian Development ment Bank, only $21 billion. So, obviously, the AIIB, the New Development Bank, and all the other banks I named, have to fill this gap. And obviously, to have such independent financial institutions, will give the developing countries, also a much greater voice in determining their own economic policy to the advantage of their own population.

Eradicating Poverty Worldwide

The aim, explicitly stated by several BRICS leaders, is to use these banks to eradicate poverty from the surface of the planet in a very short period of time. In Asia alone, you have presently over 700 million people who are still living below the poverty level. Now, Prime Minister [Narendra] Modi has made several exciting speeches, in which he declared a national objective of India, to eradicate poverty from the Indian nation.

Also, President Xi Jinping has proudly announced, repeatedly, that the Chinese economic miracle, which, nobody can deny, is one of the greatest miracles in terms of economics *ever* in the history of economies— because China was able to have an economic development in *30 years* which most industrial nations in Europe, in the United States, and elsewhere, needed 100 or even 200 years to accomplish. And Xi Jinping has announced that that kind of development, which has now transformed the poor population of the coastal regions and the southern parts of China, will be brought into the inner regions, and into the Western parts of China, which are mostly desert, and thereby—it's not so easy—to use this Chinese economic miracle as the model for the New Silk Road for every country that participates in these projects, to repeat exactly what China has accomplished.

The *Neue Zürcher Zeitung,* which is the major Swiss financial daily, had, this morning, an article with the headline, "Gold Rush Mood Thanks to the New Silk Road, Investors Are Rushing To Buy Stocks in Chinese State-Owned Enterprises. They Are Investing in the New Silk Road." I have to say that there is a certain amount of confusion in the editorial board of *Neue Zürcher Zeitung*, because they are looking at these developments with the spectacles of monetarism, but obviously, this is not what this is at all, because the AIIB, the New Development Bank, and the other institutions are *credit* institutions, and are not part of the casino economy of Wall Street, or the City of London, or Frankfurt, for that matter. But they go back very explicitly to the principles of the first Secretary of the Treasury of the United States, Alexander Hamilton, who created the first National Bank, and with that, a credit-financing institution for the real economy.

And that first National Bank, that credit system, was the basis for the gigantic industrial revolution which occurred in the United States. And it was the policy to which good American Presidents always returned, such as Lincoln, with the greenback policy; or Franklin D. Roosevelt, with the New Deal, and the Glass-Steagall separation, and the Reconstruction Finance Corporation, which happened to be not only the motor for the United States to overcome the Depression in the '30s, but it was also, in the form of the Kreditanstalt für Wiederaufbau [Reconstruction Credit Institution], the basis for the German economic miracle, in the postwar reconstruction of Germany.

This was also the basis of the proposal by Lyndon LaRouche to create an International Development Bank, which he made in 1975, and for which this organization has campaigned practically in all the years since. And we have now the development that this idea, to have a bank which is only there to finance development, is coming into reality.

The Casino's About To Blow

This is extremely urgent, because the trans-Atlantic region is based on a completely different idea, namely, the profit-maximization of the casino, and that is totally bankrupt, and it is about to go bust.

The recently published Beige Book of the Federal Reserve, which is estimated to reflect the complete denial of reality by European economists, in fact, pretends that there is an upswing in the United States, but what it shows, the real figures show—and these figures are still manipulated—is that you have a collapse of the real economy in the United States. The New York Fed's Manufacturing Index, which measures manufacturing activity in New York State, went down to negative 1.19 points, from plus 6.9 points in March. The new orders index went down from negative 2.4 points, to negative 6.0. The employment index collapsed from 18.6 to plus 9.6%. So, even by the fraudulent statistics of the Fed, the real economy is shrinking.

But the real crisis is that the too-big-to-fail banks have a derivative exposure which is today 40-80% larger than in 2008, at the point of the collapse of Lehman Brothers. And this system could detonate at any moment.

For example, if the Fed increased the interest rate just a tiny amount, that derivative bubble would, almost certainly, explode. And if the European Union contin-ues its hard line against Greece, a policy which is also supported by German Finance Minister Schäuble, and drives Greece out of the Eurozone, which is now on its way—for example, Standard & Poors just downgraded Greece from a B- to level CCC+, which is already junk bond level.

Therefore, in reality, we are looking at the upcoming explosion of the financial system of the trans-Atlantic sector, and these new banks are actually the lifeboat for a sinking *Titanic*.

The problem of the trans-Atlantic sector could be solved very easily, if the United States would go back to the Glass-Steagall separation of the banks, which was introduced by Franklin D. Roosevelt in 1933, and only repealed in 1999. That, by the way, makes the Presidential campaign of the pre-Presidential candidate Martin O'Malley *the most important campaign*, because he has said that the most urgent action he would take, if he were to be elected to the White House, would be the implementation of Glass-Steagall: Protect the commercial banks and separate the investment banks, and do not finance them any longer through quantitative easing, or through so-called rescue packages,—and they would go bankrupt, if they were forced to rely on their own system.

And there is a connection between the pending collapse of the Wall Street banks, the City of London banks, and other related banks—and the increasing war danger, which we have discussed many times. The Empire collapse is what is driven by the pending collapse of the banks, and the war danger in Ukraine and the Middle East comes from that.

Therefore, it is a life-or-death question of civilization, that we get the United States, and the European nations, to join with the BRICS, to join with the New Silk Road, and join the "win-win" perspective, as a conscious war-avoidance policy. Because if all the countries of Europe, the United States, and the BRICS countries—to which, for example, Russia belongs—work together in these large projects, then, and only then, can you overcome the reason for war.

Because war has always occurred as a result of geopolitics, and we have to get the United States off the idea of the Project for a New American Century doctrine, which was introduced by the neocons at the end of the '90s, which is the idea that they will not allow one nation, or a group of nations, to ever become stronger than the United States.

FIGURE 2

January 13, 2013

January 13, 2014

NASA/NOAA

The disappearance of snow cover in the Sierra Nevada mountains from January 2013 to January 2014.

The California Drought: A Nazi Policy

So, therefore, let's look at the reality of the situation. Not only is the trans-Atlantic sector about to experience a bigger blowout of the system than in 2008; the most dramatic situation we have right now is in California, and in the entire Southwest of the United States, where you have a prolonged drought, and a huge water shortage.

On the 12th of March, there was an op-ed in the *Los Angeles Times* by J. Famiglietti, who is from the NASA Jet Propulsion Laboratory; he said that California today has water supplies for only about one year left in its reservoirs. You can see here on this picture (**Figure 2**), the drought emptying the reservoirs and also reducing the snowpack, which means there will be no water flowing into these reservoirs and other water systems. And what was the reaction of Governor Brown? About a week ago, he announced a mandatory cut of water usage of 25%, except for agriculture, *and* fracking, this completely insane method of production of shale gas and oil.

Already over 500,000 acres remained unplanted in

the last year, and it probably will be more than 1 million acres, which will not be used for agriculture this year. Several towns in California are already out of water. And soon, you will see a migration of people out of the largest and most productive state in the United States.

So, when we, about a week ago, presented in the state legislature in Sacramento, the revolutionary new concept of how to deal with this water crisis, which has been worked out by Ben Deniston and Lyndon La-Rouche, with the science team he's working with,—we had a very unusual, shocking experience. When we presented this revolutionary proposal of Ben Deniston to Mr. O'Connor, who is the principal consultant to the State Senate Committee for Natural Resources and Water—and we went there with the expectation that they would be happy to find people concerned with solving the water crisis—the reaction was a complete hysterical denial that there were water shortages before, a cyclic development of weather patterns over thousands of years, that the drought is not the result of anthropogenic activities of mankind. He completely freaked out.

And what Ben Deniston had proposed—he will elaborate this later on himself—is that you can have a combination of measures, like desalination of ocean water, with the help of nuclear energy, in the tradition of what Roosevelt did with the Tennessee Valley Authority, like managing and changing the Colorado River, and similar proposals. But also you could revive aspects of NAWAPA [the North American Water and Power Alliance]—that is, bringing down the plentiful water from Alaska and Canada, along the Rocky Mountains, with a system of canals all the way to Mexico. Or, use the fact that 90% of all precipitation does not occur over land, but over oceans, and that you could use the ionization of moisture in the atmosphere to develop more water.

Recent studies have focused very much on the high-energy galactic, cosmic rays in controlling the ionization of the lower atmosphere, and that seems to influence the cloud formation, and also catalyzes the condensation of water vapor in the atmosphere. That method has already been tested and applied by several countries. But it was very clear that this Mr. O'Connor had absolutely no interest in even listening to these proposals. Then, by reviewing what the problem was, we found—which we had already known before, but it came now in the context of the reduction of the water use in California—that it is crystal clear what the intention is.

The same too-big-to-fail banks, which are about to blow, including the different members of the Bush family and the American multi-billionaire T. Boone Pickens, all of these people had invested, in the last 5-10 years, enormous amounts of money into everything that has to do with water: land which is over aquifers, lakes, but also water pumps, chemicals to purify water, membranes, bottled water—just everything which has to do with water—and not only in the United States, but all over the world.

So it is very clear that what they have been trying to do is to corner the water market, in order to speculate on the scarcity of water, on rising prices, totally disregarding what would be the effect of depopulation, of destruction of agriculture, of increase of food prices—and actually killing people.

FIGURE 3

MAJOR DESERTS

And there's no question that this *is* a Nazi policy, because you see the same support of Nazi policies in Ukraine. You see it in the absolutely anti-human policy of the Troika in Greece, destroying one-third of the Greek economy; and you see it in the absolutely horrendous condition of the developing countries.

Now, the consequence which these people take into account, is the death of millions and millions of poor people.

Here you see the world deserts (**Figure 3**), which actually grow from the Atlantic Coast of Africa, all the way through the Sahel Zone, the Sahara, the Arabian peninsula, the Middle East—all the way to China, and naturally in the Southwest of America. But there are two completely different approaches to how you deal with that.

You have the speculation on the scarcity of water, on the side of Wall Street and the City of London, and other speculators.

China and India: The Counter-Example

But then if you contrast that with what China has been doing, China has, in recent years, developed the two largest water projects in the world (**Figure 4**). There is, on the one side, the Three Gorges Dam, which changed the water of the Yangtze, and has turned this into the largest power-production facility in the world, producing 22.5 gigawatts per year, and it has protected thousands of people from drowning every year, and established efficient flood control. And secondly, you

FIGURE 4

South-North Water Diversion Project

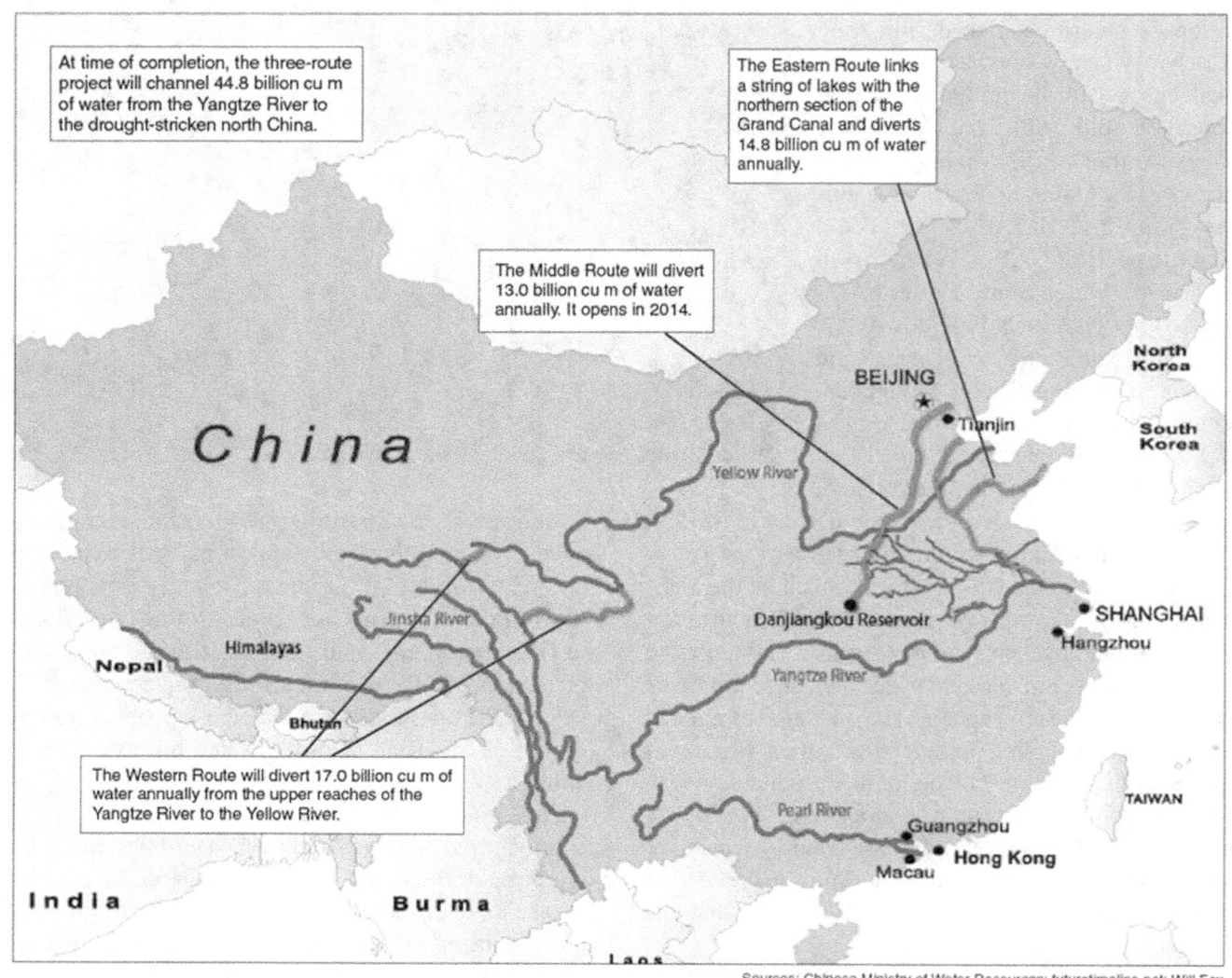

At time of completion, the three-route project will channel 44.8 billion cu m of water from the Yangtze River to the drought-stricken north China.

The Eastern Route links a string of lakes with the northern section of the Grand Canal and diverts 14.8 billion cu m of water annually.

The Middle Route will divert 13.0 billion cu m of water annually. It opens in 2014.

The Western Route will divert 17.0 billion cu m of water annually from the upper reaches of the Yangtze River to the Yellow River.

Sources: Chinese Ministry of Water Resources; futuretimeline.net; Will Fox

have the South-North Water Transfer Diversion Program, of which two of the three parts have already been completed.

Now, you see here the Eastern Route of this project, which brings water from the very water-rich spring region of the Yangtze River, to Anhui, Shandong and Jiansu provinces, filling up, on the one side, the Yellow River, and using irrigation from there. And then, secondly, the you see the Middle Route, which brings water to Beijing and Tianjin. These two routes are already bringing large amounts of water to the dry areas, while the Western Route is still in the phase of planning.

But China is not the only country that is taking this

productive approach. At the recent SAARC summit, Indian Prime Minister Modi presented a similar program for India. It is the idea of linking the Sharda River, which flows in the Himalayas, and bringing it north to south along the India-Nepal border, and bringing waters of the Yamuna River, which goes from west to the east, into the Ganga [Ganges] River Valley.

And all of this goes back to the Indira Gandhi National Water Development Authority, which she established in 1982. This was the time when we were working with her, together, on a 40-year development perspective for India. And this was not carried out, because of her assassination, but it was a gigantic project,—which had the idea of having 30 rivers linked through canals, creating 3,000 storage structures, projects which would create 34 gigawatts of hydropower,— and which would have provided 35 million hectares of land for agricultural use. It would have transferred 175 billion cubic meters of water per year, and massively increased the food production, and protected the population against floods and droughts.

Prime Minister Modi has revived all of this, and he has created a task force on the interlinking of these rivers. He announced plans to convert 101 rivers into transport channels, which will cut transport costs by 30%, and increase the capacity gigantically. That goes together with several desalination plants on the coast of Tamil Nadu, and it also involves a plan to connect 14 rivers from the Himalayas to 16 others across the Indian peninsula, adding 35 million hectares of irrigated land, and 34,000 megawatts of electricity. That is three times as much as you need to provide electricity for New York City.

Obviously, there are many, many areas in the world which need the approach taken by China and India, and which is lacking right now in California.

For example, the same approach must be taken for the Aral Sea, which has shrunk to only 5% [of its former size]. This is creating immense tensions between Tajikistan and Kyrgyzstan, which have access to several rivers before they flow on to Kazakhstan, Turkmenistan, and Uzbekistan, and naturally tensions exist between these countries.

This approach must be taken to Lake Chad, which has shrunk to less than 10% of its previous levels, and for which we have proposed for a very long time, the Transaqua plan (**Figure 5**), which was worked out by the Italian physicist Dr. [Marcello] Vichi, which has the idea of taking the abundant water—actually, too much water—from the Congo River, and bringing it up through a system of channels and canals into Lake Chad, which would transform the life of millions of people. Obviously, this is not an option, but a bitter necessity.

Because right now, we hear every week, the horrendous reports about thousands of people trying to flee across the Mediterranean, from Africa, and also from Syria and Iraq, and many hundreds of them are drowning every week. And the EU has nothing better to do than to chase these people back, and to try to prevent them from coming, which underlines once more, the complete moral bankruptcy of the EU.

FIGURE 5
The Transaqua Plan

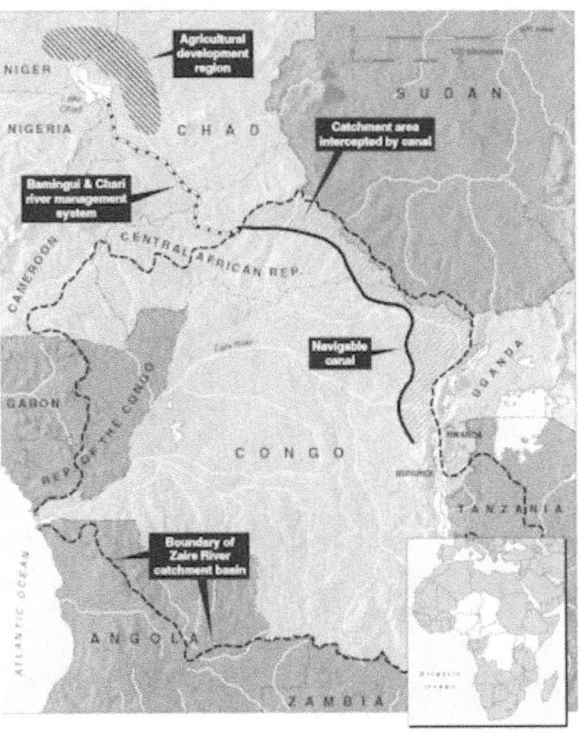

The World Land-Bridge

Now, the World Land-Bridge: This proposal, which we have produced in a study of over a year's duration, and which we published at the end of last year. This is a 370-page study, which not only outlines all the future projects, the tunnels, bridges, corridors, etc., which are needed to turn the present world situation into a coherent, connected World Land-Bridge; it also has a lot of the scientific conceptions provided by the scientific method of Mr. LaRouche, of physical economy, of why an increase in the energy-flux density in the production process, *is* the absolutely necessary way to go; and why only with these principles, can you provide food and livelihood for the increased population in the world, and that the increase in the relative population density is the law of the universe. And all of that you will find in this report.

If you look at the various projects (**Figure 6**), which I only want to identify here very, very briefly: it is a network of bridges, tunnels, and canals connecting the five continents of the world, actually turning it into a coherent world transport and infrastructure system, so that in a few years, you could travel, for example, from the

FIGURE 6

The World Land-Bridge Network—Key Links and Corridors

*Committed, underway or completed.

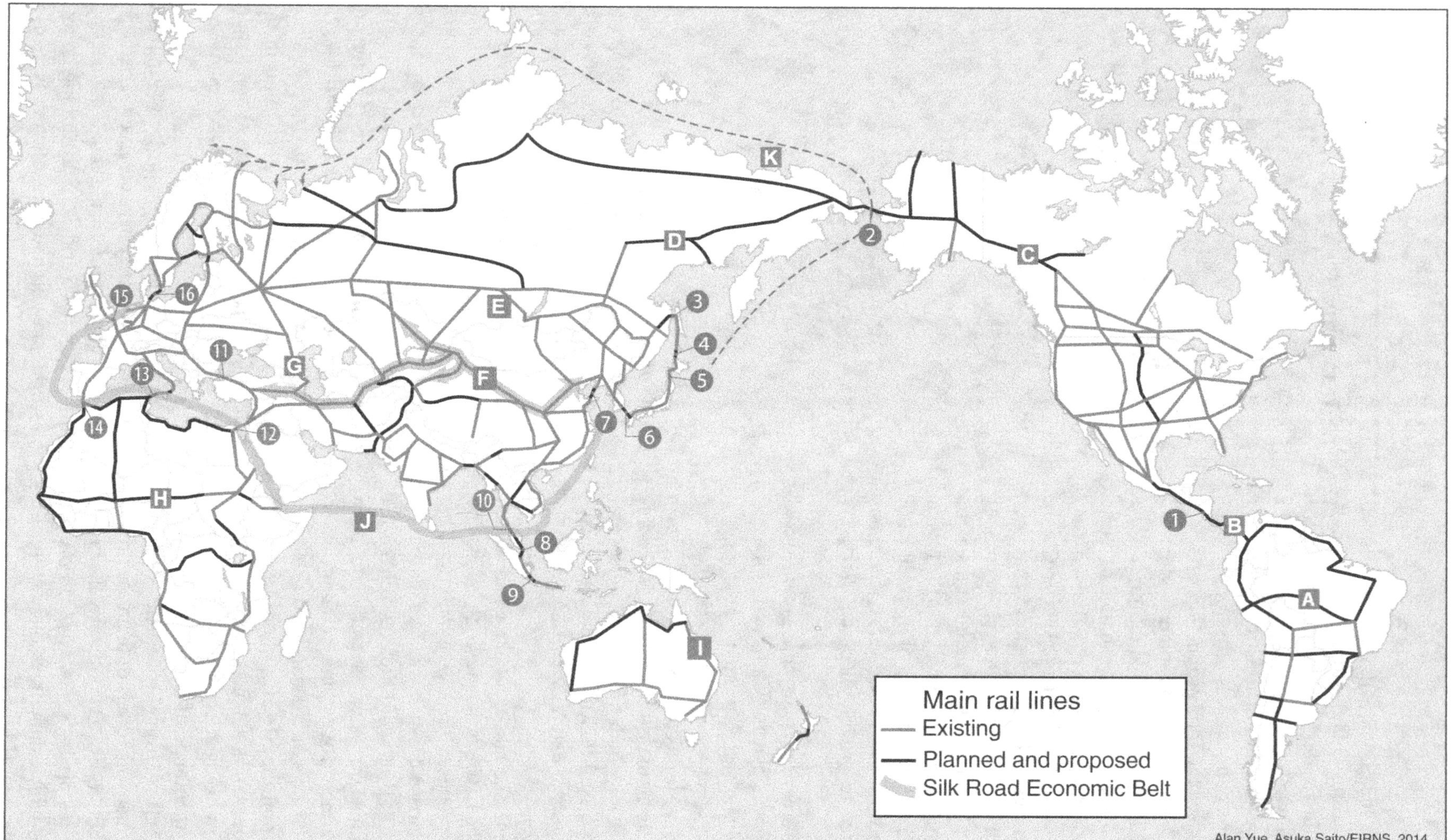

Alan Yue, Asuka Saito/EIRNS, 2014

Main rail lines
— Existing
— Planned and proposed
▬ Silk Road Economic Belt

CORRIDORS
A *Peru-Brazil Transcontinental Railway
B *Darien Gap Inter-American Railway
C *Alaska-Canada-Lower 48 Rail Line
D The Bering Strait Connector
E *Trans-Siberian Corridors
F *Silk Road Economic Belt
G *International North-South Transport
   Corridor
H *Cross Africa Rail Lines
I *Australia Ring Railway
J *Maritime Silk Road
K *Northern Sea Route

Note: Geographical locations and corridors are shown schematically, with more than one railway combined as a single line in cases where major routes are parallel and in proximity. Maps within chapters of this report show greater detail.

LINKS
1 *Great Inter-Oceanic Canal, Nicaragua
2 Bering Strait Tunnel
3 Sakhalin Island-Mainland (Russia)
   Connection
4 Sakhalin-Hokkaido Tunnel
5 *Seikan Tunnel
6 Japan-Korea Undersea Tunnel
7 *Bohai Tunnel
8 Strait of Malacca Bridge
9 Sunda Strait Bridge
10 Isthmus of Kra Canal
11 *Bosporus Strait Rail Tunnel
12 *Suez Canal Expansion
13 Italy-Tunisia Link
14 Strait of Gibraltar Tunnel
15 *English Channel Tunnel
16 *Scandinavian-Continental Links

FIGURE 7
FIGURE 7
The Bering Strait Tunnel

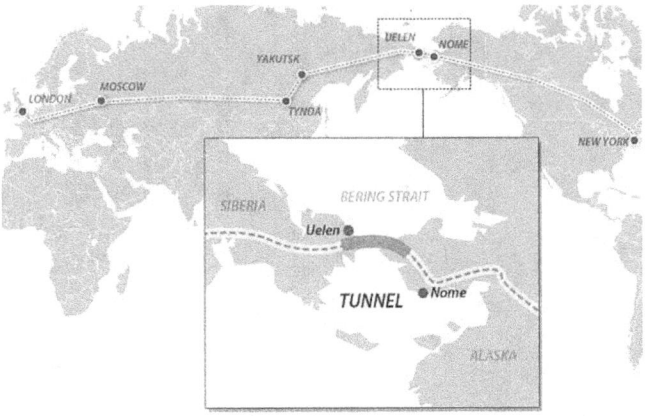

Russian Railways Vladimir Yakunin has proposed building a high-speed railway from London, across the Bering Strait, and from there, to New York.

southern tip of South America, by maglev train, all the way up through the Americas, through the Bering Strait, all the way to Cape of Good Hope in Africa, or to Indonesia, if you want to take a different route; and that would be faster than going by ship presently.

These projects include, for example: the second Panama Canal, which has started to be built in Nicaragua—this is here, number 1 on the map (Figure 6). This already started last December, with the help of China. It's a 278-kilometer canal. Then, number 2, is the building of the Bering Strait tunnel (**Figure 7**). This was recently proposed by the head of Russian Railways Vladimir Yakunin, which is to built a fast railway system from London all the way to the Bering Strait, and from there, to New York. And that has been adopted as the official policy of Russia.

Now obviously, what is lacking right now is the American commitment, but I think that that is what we are campaigning for, to be adopted.

Number 3 on this map (Figure 6) is the tunnel connecting the Sakhalin Island with the Russian mainland, which is intended to be a tunnel of 7.3 kilometers. Number 4, the Sakhalin-Hokkaido tunnel, or bridge, which will be 45 kilometers. Number 7 is the tunnel connecting the shores of Bohai Bay, shortening the distance to 100 kilometers, connecting two Chinese cities, Dalian and Yantai. Number 10 is the building of the Kra Canal, which is intended to be an alternative to the Malacca Strait, which is completely

FIGURE 8
Mediterranean Basin Great Infrastructure Projects

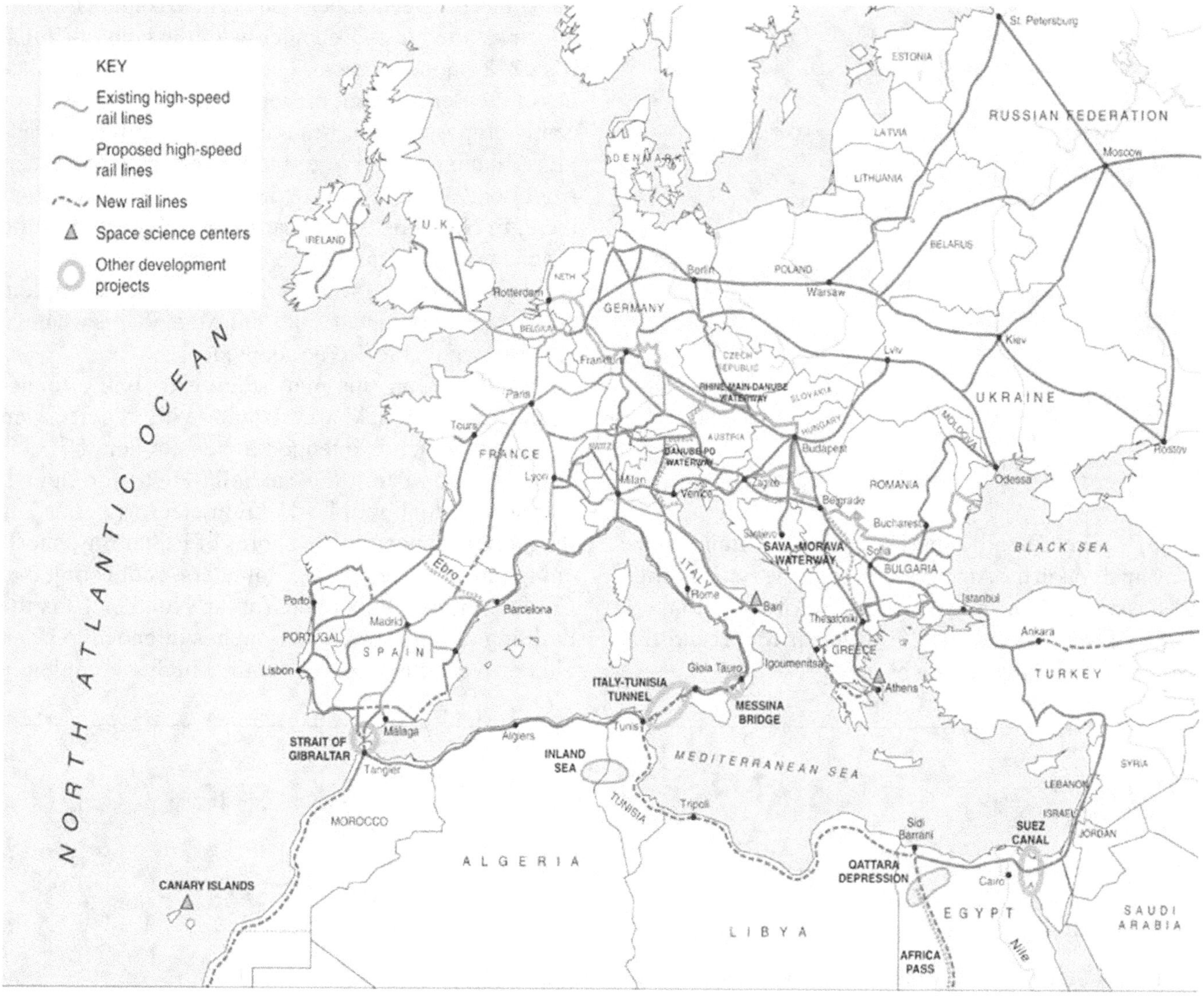

overworked. Number 12 is the expansion of the Suez Canal, which is happening at a very fast speed, under the leadership of the new el-Sisi government in Egypt, which has completely transformed that country, and caused total excitement among the population.

This is the European extension of the Eurasian Land-Bridge (**Figure 8**), a part of the World Land-Bridge, which we produced in 2012, when it became clear that the policy of the Troika had transformed all of Southern Europe—Greece, Italy, Spain, Portugal—into economic desert zones, reducing the real economy of Greece, for example, by one-third, causing

two-thirds unemployment of the youth, increasing the death rate, and increasing the suicide rate. The picture is the same for Italy and Spain and Portugal. And it was the idea of extending the New Silk Road/Eurasian Land-Bridge into Spain, into the Balkans, and then from there, building bridges and tunnels into Africa, and connecting it with the extension of the New Silk Road into Africa.

This is all in the documents of EIR Special Report *The New Silk Road Becomes the World Land-Bridge*, and I can only advise you, that you should acquire this report, because this is the blueprint for the next decades of human civilization.

In the Confucian tradition, Zepp-LaRouche said, there is the "idea that the laws of the universe must be a guidance for our political order on the planet."

The Principles To Be Followed

Now, Xi Jinping announced at the Boao conference the principles of this new policy, which basically are the five principles of the Bandung Conference of the Non-Aligned Movement from 1955. It is in complete cohesion with the UN Charter. It is based on respect for international law. It is the idea of non-interference, respect for the sovereignty of the other country, the respect for the difference in the social system of the other country, and to basing the policy on the maximum development of the other—which happens to be also the principles of the Peace of Westphalia, and international law.

Xi Jinping made a speech on that occasion, where he said, "We have only one planet, and countries share one world. To do well in Asia, and the world, we cannot do without each other. What China needs most is a harmonious and stable domestic environment, and a peaceful and tranquil international environment. Turbulence or war run against the fundamental interest of the Chinese people. China has suffered from turbulence and war for more than a century, since modern times. and the Chinese people would never want to inflict the same tragedy on other countries, or peoples.

"History has taught us that no country that tried to achieve its goal with force ever succeeded."

The proof of that, obviously, is the condition of Iraq, of Syria, of Libya, of Ukraine, and many other countries,—in Africa, for example.

What we have to accomplish, therefore, is to make an all-out effort to convince the United States and the European nations that they should join with the BRICS, and with the New Silk Road policy.

I believe that we have come to a point in human history, where either we bring the political and economic order into cohesion with the real laws of the universe, of the physical universe, or we are threatened with extinction in a nuclear annihilation. However, I think that in all great traditions, you have this idea that the laws of the universe must be a guidance for our political order on the planet.

You find that idea beautifully developed in the Confucian tradition, of 2,500 years of Chinese history,— the idea that politics must follow the Mandate of Heaven, that there must be a harmony of all nations based on the idea of Love, which is the Confucian notion of *ren*, and that each nation must fulfill its rightful place, and its rightful task in this alliance, which is the notion of *li*.

That same idea you find in Hinduism, that the cosmic order must be implemented on the planet, in the political order. You find it also in the Christian humanist tradition of European culture, of which, after all, America is a part. It's based on the idea that concordance in the macrocosm can only exist if all microcosms develop in an appropriate fashion and way, promoting the interest of the other as if it were their own.

So, I think we have an unbelievably optimistic situation. It is full of dangers. We are threatened with World War III, very immediately, but the solution is there. I mean, if we get the United States to really become a republic again, as it was intended by the Founding Fathers, as it was established by Alexander Hamilton and this idea of a National Bank and a credit system; as it was promoted by John Quincy Adams, who had his idea that America must be a republic in an alliance of sovereign republics; as it was reconstituted by Abraham Lincoln; and by Franklin D. Roosevelt, and as it was echoed by John F. Kennedy.

I think we have to revive that American tradition, and then I think Europe will follow, because, as you could see with the rush into the AIIB, and the excitement about Modi, about China in general, in Europe,— I think we could really turn the tide. And I want to ask all of you, to join in this effort.